TWO SCOTS PLAYS

TWO SCOTS PLAYS

By

ALEXANDER REID

COLLINS

ST JAMES'S PLACE, LONDON

1958

The plays included in this volume are copyright and no performance or public reading of them may be given unless a licence has been obtained in advance from the author's agents, Messrs. Curtis Brown Ltd., 13 King Street, Covent Garden, London, W.C. 2.

© ALEXANDER REID, 1958
PRINTED IN GREAT BRITAIN
COLLINS CLEAR-TYPE PRESS : LONDON AND GLASGOW

Contents

Foreword

THE TWO plays which follow, anglicised versions of plays originally written in Braid Scots with the aim of their performance in the first instance by the bi-lingual players of the Glasgow Citizens Theatre, were made by acting, somewhat belatedly, on a suggestion of Mr. Ivor Brown's in his *Observer* review of a Citizens revival of *The Lass* at Perth.

In that review, and later elsewhere, Mr. Brown suggested that if my work, 'The Scots of which would baffle an English audience,' could be put into 'near English' it would find an audience elsewhere, and when eventually I screwed myself up to the task of rewriting them this forecast was proved correct in the sense that both plays printed here became exportable—first into England, later abroad. *The Lass wi' the Muckle Mou'* indeed will shortly reach its fourth continent and as I write it is being translated into Serbo-Croat.

In anglicising the plays two possibilities were open to me. One was to rewrite them in the best 'English English' I could muster; the other to take advantage of the large number of words which Scots and English have in common and while keeping as close as possible to the original speech rhythms and construction, to delete all specifically

ix

Scots words except very common ones, or those, the meaning of which was made clear by their place in the context. It was, as will be seen, the second course that I finally plumped for, and not only for sentimental reasons.

Scots English—except in exceptional cases—stems not out of life but out of literature. At its best, as in R. L. Stevenson, it smells of printer's ink and the English Literature class. It is written out of our educated heads and not out of our whole personalities and it speaks to the head and not to the whole person. It is dictionary English, useful for asking a direction in London or gossiping about the poetry of T. S. Eliot at the Aldeburgh Festival, but because it leaves the heart untouched it is almost valueless for literary purposes, and especially for poetic purposes. Nor can this be otherwise for though Scotland and England have a vast number of words in common, the Scots and English overtones of many words are quite startlingly different. Consider only one example, the word river. For most Scots, the word river conjures up the image of amber-hued frothing torrent, full of salmon and trout, dashing down among boulders from dark and rugged mountains on the peaks of which patches of snow linger for the greater part of the year. All Scottish rivers are not like this, but many are, and that is the type image—an image suggesting loneliness, mystery, primeval nature. But in England on the other hand the typical associations of the word river are utterly different from this. There, over most of the country, the word river evokes the sort of landscape through which wind slow flowing streams like the Cam and the Ouse, and the associations are with fat-cows-in-rich-meadows, flowery gardens, strawberry-teason-the-vicarage-lawn, and, in general, a comfortable domesticity.

Scots writers can of course, if they are industrious enough, learn to use English words for their English instead of their Scottish overtones (as we can learn to use French for French life, as opposed to French dictionary, meanings) but this is the job of a life-time and those who devote themselves to it are usually too old, by the time they have learned to play the instrument, to be capable of composing anything new for it. Moreover, the fact that when working in English English we are using an alien tongue has in many cases (and very obviously in my own) an inhibiting effect on the imagination. I have written six plays to date of which three are (for the most part) in the best English I could muster and three are almost wholly in Scots, and the difference between the two groups of plays goes far deeper than a difference of language. All three plays in the English group are satires or *pièces-à-thèse* : that is they are addressed to the intellect and not to the feelings except in so far as these are worked on through structure rather than words. The three Scots plays, on the other hand (whatever English criticism may make of them) undoubtedly " work " on all levels for Scottish audiences, and were written out of my whole self for the whole selves of others. I could not if my life had hung on it, have written any of these plays directly into English in the first instance ; not even into the anglicised Scots in which two of them appear here.

There is besides another reason why it seemed desirable to keep as near to the originals as possible.

The Scottish dramatist, so far as his intentions are

serious, is not, as so many people still seem to think, trying to write an English kind of play about Scotland or elsewhere in Scots. He is trying to make an original Scottish contribution to world drama which will be as distinct from the English contribution as the English contribution is from the French, American or Russian, and to depart more than is necessary from the original verbal form of these plays would, in my own view, be to betray this aim. Scottish literature and the Scottish use of language can be separated in theory but not in practice. For two hundred years we have been trying to write like Englishmen and at the end of it we can only say with enormous labour what a native English writer, otherwise of equal power, says spontaneously out of nature. It is a brute fact that Scotland has not produced one literary artist of world importance since Burns and Scott and it is another brute fact that everything Burns wrote in English is third rate and everything Scott wrote in English is pedestrian. All the lasting work of these men was written in Scots. To write first-rate English English is, to be blunt about it, almost as difficult for a Scot as writing *Tam o' Shanter* or *Le Cimetière Marin* would be for an Englishman.

When I first (as a youngster in my teens) visited France (a country incidentally, where now I have spent a month for every day I have spent in England) I lived for the first three days almost entirely on omelettes, bread and wine. To order anything more elaborate was beyond my powers of communication. Something equivalent to this has happened to Scots writers since they began to work in English. They have written not so much what they wanted to write but what they were able to write and the result was not always so interesting. The return to Scots is a return to meaning and sincerity. We can only grow from our own roots and our roots are not English.

What I have written above is I believe true of Scottish writing in general, but it has a particular importance for the dramatists associated with our young but growing theatre.

A British Theatre does not exist and never has existed. There is an English Theatre, and a French Theatre, and a Russian Theatre, and a Chinese Theatre, but we up here in the wind and the rain are neither English nor French, Russian or Chinese. If we are to fulfil our hope that Scotland may some day make a contribution to World Drama as individual and valuable as that made by Norway in the nineteenth and by Ireland in the present century, we can only do so by cherishing, not repressing our national peculiarities (including our language), though whether a Scottish National Drama, if it comes to birth, will be written in Braid Scots or the speech, redeemed for literary purposes, of Argyle Street, Glasgow, or the Kirkgate, Leith, is anyone's guess. That it will be written in some sort of Scots however is quite certain. A National Drama cannot be created in a language foreign to the people from whom it springs and the spoken language of Scotland, whatever name we give to it, is not standard English.

To sum up, Scots dramatists to-day are writing in Scots not for chauvinistic reasons but for exactly the same reason that English dramatists write in English and French dramatists in French : because that is the way that comes naturally to them ; and because only by working within their national tradition (though this, with our minute population, condemns us to poverty) can they produce their best work. It would be fine if we could write equally well in English but most of us cannot.

The root of the Scottish literary revival is a humble recognition that we are what we are and must make the best of that. For myself I do not think that either what we are or the culture we belong to needs any apology.

My own first play, a satirical comedy, was written in English English, set in London and first performed at the Lyceum, Edinburgh, by the English actors of the Wilson Barrett Repertory Company which was for many years the only resident theatre company in Edinburgh. Though it did not reach London it got far enough over the border to suggest that it would be wise to develop this vein and hope to go farther on the next occasion. But fate, temperament, a Braid Scots childhood and the rise of the Glasgow Citizens Theatre decided otherwise. Before I could take another step on the well-worn road that runs to the south, I got a beguiling flash of the eye from a lowland lass standing at the mouth of a Cannongait Close in my native city. Her shoes were of Midland make, her frock from Japan, her stockings were a gift, I think, of a passing G.I. But about her head and shoulders, to shield her from the pelting of the Edinburgh rain, she had wrapped the dark tartan shawl of a Highland grandmother, and on her lips, smeared with Woolworth's lipstick, was a speech not so different yet from the speech in which worked Burns and Fergusson and the great and anonymous poets who made the Border Ballads. It was that speech that got me; it was irresistible, and like the Scots-born American, Paul Jones, at Pittsburg, during the War of Independence, I said, " To hell with the British ! "—and followed the maid of the region. *The Lass wi' the Muckle Mou'* and *The World's Wonder* are fruits of that meeting. I wrote the original versions of both these plays with great pleasure. I hope that some of that pleasure will reach the reader now. Structurally the versions printed here are identical with the originals except that the present opening scene of *The World's Wonder* was not staged in the first productions of the play either in Scotland or England.

ALEXANDER REID

Edinburgh 1957

THE LASS WI' THE MUCKLE MOU'

MUCKLE MOU'

or

Once Upon a Rhyme

A Comedy

To

JAMES CRAMPSEY

who knows how it began

CHARACTERS

THOMAS THE RHYMER	*a ballad-writer*
THE LADY IN GREEN	*an immortal*
SIR GIDEON MURRAY	*a border Baron*
LADY GRIZEL MURRAY	*his wife*
MEG MURRAY	*their daughter*
LIZZY	*a maid-servant*
WILLIE SCOTT	*a cattle thief*
WATTIE	*a retainer*
JOCK	*another*
RAB	*a drunkard*
WILLIE'S FATHER	*(voice only)*

First performed, by permission of Glasgow Citizens Theatre, by the East Lothian Repertory Company, at Dunbar, October 24, 1950.

THE LADY IN GREEN	Phoebe Stobie
THOMAS THE RHYMER	James Ross
SIR GIDEON MURRAY	William Nimmo
MEG MURRAY	Mary Anderson
GRIZEL MURRAY	Roberta Greig
WILLIE SCOTT	William Carr
WATTIE	James Vance
LIZZIE	May Henderson
JOCK	Alexander Ross
RAB	David Barrie

Producer : William H. Campbell

First performed by Glasgow Citizens Theatre, at the Gaiety Theatre, Ayr, November 20, 1950.

THE LADY IN GREEN	Rona Anderson
THOMAS THE RHYMER	Roddy MacMillan
SIR GIDEON MURRAY	Eric Woodburn
MEG MURRAY	Sheila Latimer
GRIZEL MURRAY	Madeleine Christie
WILLIE SCOTT	Douglas Campbell
WATTIE	Andrew Keir
LIZZIE	Pat Goldie
JOCK	Ian MacNaughton
RAB	Abe Barker

Producer : John Casson

ACT ONE

SCENE ONE : A woodland glade near Elibank Castle,
transformed without intermission into
SCENE TWO : The hall at Elibank.

ACT TWO

SCENE ONE : The hall at Elibank, half an hour later.
SCENE TWO : The Elibank Dungeon, the same night.

ACT THREE

SCENE : The Elibank battlements, in the early
morning, two days later.

ACT I

Moonlight : Where Elfland touches the world in a glade in the wood near Elibank Castle in the Borderland of the Balladists. Silhouetted against the sky are some ancient trees, and embedded in the turf in the foreground is a mossy boulder. An owl hoots softly and faint elusive harp music is heard. The owl hoots a second time and into the glade enter Thomas the Rhymer and The Lady in Green. Thomas, dressed in jerkin and hose, wears a plumed hat and has a harp slung about his shoulders. Any age between thirty-five and forty, he is tall and thin, with an eager yet humorous face, and is full of assurance for he is the greatest poet of his day and well aware of it. The Lady in Green is dressed as described in the ballad and there is a touch of mischief in her majesty. For the moment however she is serious, even a little sad, for Thomas is leaving her.

THE LADY IN GREEN : Well, Thomas, here we are at the land of the living and at my land's end. There lies the world you hankered for and I hope you like it !

THOMAS : [*Taking a deep breath*] I like it fine, lady. My, I'd forgot what a grand smell earth has to it. You could almost make a meal of it ! There's grass in it, and dung in it, and byre-stink and the Lord kens what else !

THE L.I.G. : There's churchyard mould, Thomas. Don't forget that ! And the sour-sweet smell of the robber's corpses on the hanging shaw. Don't forget them, Thomas !

9

THOMAS : It's the salt of the dish, lady ! It would lack all savour without it. [*An owl hoots*] Losh ! Did you hear yon ? Yon was the screech of a hunting hoolit or I never heard one. Oh, the pleasure it'll be to go hunting again ! [*He freezes*] Ah, but what was that ?

THE L.I.G. : The death squeal of the hunted mouse when the hoolit gripped it. That's a common sound in the earth world too, Thomas—and not a bonny one !

THOMAS : It makes you grue to listen to it ! But ach, you'll not frighten me with a squeaking mouse. It hangs together. Harried and harrier, pleasure and pain—there's no divorcing them this side of mortality.

THE L.I.G. : No, but you can live above them with me, Thomas—if you're willing.

THOMAS : I'm sorry, lady. I'm not ready for it yet as a steady thing. There's a deal of the old Adam awake in me yet—as you should ken.

THE L.I.G. : Sometimes I wonder if it's not for that, that I like you ! But what's the matter with you now— staring about there like a mazed calf at a fair ?

THOMAS : [*Looking about him, puzzled*] This isn't the bank at Huntlie ?

THE L.I.G. : Huntlie ? You're far from Huntlie ! This is the old wood behind the castle of Elibank—Murray's castle.

THOMAS : How came we here ?

THE L.I.G. : You didn't imagine yon was the only gate in the Borders, did you ?

THOMAS : Isn't it, then ?

THE L.I.G. : There's a gate to yon land on every hillside, Thomas. Aye ! and behind every tree in the wood—if you've eyes to see them. But enough of blethers! There's a cold wind blows about the cross-ways of the worlds that's ill to bear, and I must away. Will you not come back with me, lad? Come on! Give up this daft notion of yours and stay on with me as you have for these seven years gone.

THOMAS: Lady, I must write that ballad.

THE L.I.G.: Is there no matter for a ballad in the glens of Elfland?

THOMAS: I'm sorry, lady, but somehow I've no will to compose there. There's no conflict in Elfland—and what's art without conflict? And there's no pathos— and what's a ballad if it lacks pathos? No, no, lady, Elfland's a grand place to live, but the place for poetry's on earth. Besides I ken just the story I want now.

THE L.I.G.: Oh?

THOMAS: Aye, I've got it all charted out in my head. I want a story—a true one, mark you!—that begins with some sort of a struggle—a ding-dong fight if possible. Then, besides that, I need a good dollop of sentiment, for the women, you know—that's the one thing that interests them! Next, I'd like a grand climax in which the key character has to make a desperate choice between true glory and mere worldly considerations. And finally I need a pathetic ending—because that's my speciality!

THE L.I.G.: And you think you'll find a story like that ready waiting for you on earth?

THOMAS: There's not a doubt of it! The country's fair hotching with such stories. It's the pattern of life in the world!

THE L.I.G.: There's been a deal of changes in the world

since last you walked in it, Thomas. Maybe the pattern's changed!

THOMAS: I'll never believe it! I'll tell you what, lady, I'll wager you another seven year's bonded service against another kiss that within seven days I'll find such a story and wrought it into the finest ballad ever carped in the Borders—which is just the same as saying in the whole wide world! And every word of it will be true.

THE L.I.G.: True as the world kens it or as we ken it?

THOMAS: True both as the world and as we ken it. It'll be a plain account of events as they're acted out on the earth, made glorious by noble language. My language!

THE L.I.G.: I'll take your wager! [*They each lick their right thumbs and touch these together, then lick their left thumbs and touch these*] And just to make certain sure you remember the compact I'll put a wee harmless spell on you. [*She draws herself erect and becomes majestic*] Thomas the Rhymer, I send you back to the lying world with the tongue that must never lie! [*As the spell takes effect Thomas sways and then staggers back, looking horrified*] What's the matter with you now?

THOMAS: Lady, do you ken what you just said?

THE L.I.G.: Aye, fine I do.

THOMAS: You mean I must *always* speak truth?

THE L.I.G.: Just that, Thomas.

THOMAS: *All* the time, lady?

THE L.I.G.: Aye, Thomas. From this night onwards.

THOMAS: [*In great distress*] Lady, it's not possible! You—you don't know what it's like down there. I wouldn't dare open my mouth with such a curse on me. How

12

could I buy or sell or pass a word with a lass with such a handicap? Take back your spell, lady. Take it back or I'll have to throw the whole thing up!

THE L.I.G. : And that's the world that you're yearning for! Very well, I'll compromise with you. In the ordinary affairs of the day I'll allow you the customary latitude, but in all that affects the making of this ballad, and the ballad itself—not an inch, Thomas! not a syllable! And remember, I'll be watching you!

THOMAS : [*Relieved*] Oh, that's all right. I've no fears about the ballad. It was the general curse that shook me. Thank you, lady.

THE L.I.G. : Don't thank me too soon! And now " True Thomas " before we part, will you do me one last service?

THOMAS : Aye, surely. You've but to name it.

THE L.I.G. : Will you carp over just once more, the start of the ballad you made about me?

THOMAS : With pleasure, lady! Sit you there while I find my note.

> [*The Lady sits on the stone while Thomas unslings his harp, strikes a chord and sings*]

" True Thomas lay on Huntlie Bank
A ferlie he spied wi' his e'e ;
And there he saw a ladye bright
Come riding down by the Eildon tree.

" Her skirt was o' the grass-green silk
Her mantle o' the velvet fine
At ilka tett o' her horse's mane
Hung fifty silver bells and nine.

" True Thomas he pu'd aff his cap
    [*Thomas does so*]
And louted low down on his knee
    [*He does so while the Lady rises*]
' Hail to thee, Mary, Queen o' Heaven !
For thy peer on earth could never be ! '

THE L.I.G. : [*Sings, stepping away a little*]
' Oh, no ! Oh no ! Thomas,' she said,
' That name does not belong to me.
I'm but the Queen of fair Elfland
That am hither come to visit thee.
    [*She comes back and puts a hand on his shoulders*]

" ' Harp and carp, Thomas,' she said
' Harp and carp along with me.
And if ye dare to kiss my lips,
Sure of your bodie I will be ! '

THOMAS : [*Rising*]
' Betide me well betide me woe
That weird shall never daunten me ! '
    [*He steps towards her but she retreats*]
Syne he has kissed her rosy lips
All underneath the Eildon tree.

THE L.I.G. : [*Taking Thomas's hand : Sings*]
' Now ye must gang with me,' she said
' True Thomas ye must gang wi' me,
And ye must serve me seven years
Through well and woe as may chance to be.' "
    [*She breaks off*]

Oh Thomas, Thomas ! The seven years are gone but I'm sweir sweir to lose you !
    [*Thomas backs in alarm and she follows him*]

Will I cast a glamoury over you, Thomas? Will I make you get down on your knees and beg me to take you back?

THOMAS: [*Kneeling*] Your Majesty! You promised you'd let me go if I wanted. . . .

THE L.I.G.: Aye, but I didn't think that you'd want! Still, I must keep the compact. If you'll not stay willing I'll never make you. But mind, lad, when you find the woesome ways of the wearysome world too much for you —I'll always be here.

THOMAS: [*Rising*] Could I forget you!

[*He kisses her hand and then turns to go but she calls him back*]

THE L.I.G.: Thomas!

THOMAS: Aye, lady?

THE L.I.G.: I think if you went down to the Murrays' house you might find the makings of the ballad you're seeking.

THOMAS: Thank you, lady. I'll look in there.

[*Again he turns to go and again she calls to him*]

THE L.I.G.: And Thomas . . .

THOMAS: Aye?

THE L.I.G.: Haste you back, Thomas!

THOMAS: That I will, lady—when I've writ my ballad!

[*Thomas goes off to the right, the Queen of Elfland smiling after him. Then she turns to go off left and at the same time the light in the woods fades quickly down and the glade is transformed into Scene Two, the Hall of the Castle of Elibank—a large stone-walled room, furnished with a long table, two armchairs, some rough wooden settles and stools and a tapestry frame, and with its walls*] *decorated with arms, armour and hunting trophies. There is one door into the kitchen premises and another into the gate-tower and so to the exterior. To the right a huge open fireplace with a chain hanging down the chimney to which a huge black pot, bubbling over the hearth fire, is hooked. The window is shuttered. Seated in the centre of the hall is Sir Gideon Murray, a blanket about his shoulders and his feet in a tub of hot water. He is about to sneeze. He does sneeze, hugely, then cranes round to shout towards the kitchen]*

SIR G. : Grizel! [*There is no answer and after a pause he tries again*] Grizel, woman! [*There is still no answer and now Sir Gideon half rises and roars like a bull*] Grizel! I want you!

> [*Grizel enters hastily from the kitchen. She is a woman of about fifty and would be handsome but for her rather big mouth. She wears a long woollen dress and over it a voluminous white apron. Her sleeves are rolled up and her hands and arms whitened with flour*]

GRIZEL : Now, what is it?

SIR G. : There's more heat in a wet well-stone than in this water. You might put a drop more in, Grizel.

GRIZEL : [*Taking jug from table and going to pot for hot water*] Can you not help yourself, Gideon? You ken, I'm busy.

SIR G. : Do you want me to get my death walking about the flags on my bare feet? I thought you cared more for me, Grizel?

GRIZEL : [*Irritably*] I've got the supper to make and I can't be running back and forth between here and the kitchen every half-minute. [*Pours water into tub*] There! Will that suit you?

16

SIR G. : [*After testing it cautiously with one toe*] It's not very warm yet.

GRIZEL : [*Going for second jugful*] Tit! You're a terrible nuisance, Gideon. If you're ill you should be in your bed. [*Splashes water into tub*] Will that do?

> [*Sir Gideon experiments gingerly and withdraws his foot quickly. He looks up at Grizel dubiously*]

GRIZEL : What's the matter with you now?

SIR G. : It's fair scalding now, Grizel.

GRIZEL : [*Drawing herself up*] Oh!—You! You're worse than a parcel of bairns. Now I'll have to get you some cold, I suppose!

> [*Enter Meg from kitchen, a well-shaped pleasant-looking girl but with an even bigger mouth than her mother*]

MEG : Is anything wrong, Mother?

GRIZEL : Just your father! Run through and fetch a jug of cold water from the kitchen, Meg.

MEG : Aye, Mother [*Exit Meg*].

SIR G. : [*Plaintively*] I'm sorry to be such a nuisance to you, Grizel.

GRIZEL : And so you should be! [*Looking with disapproval at water splashed about floor*] Losh! What a mess you've made. The place is fair swimming. [*Calling to kitchen*] Lizzy!

> [*Enter Lizzy from the kitchen. Lizzy is a young servant girl of about eighteen. She is what in Scotland they call " glaiket," not a half-wit but moving that way*]

LIZZY : Did you want me, lady?

GRIZEL : What else for would I be shouting on you? Bring a wash-cloth.

LIZZY : Aye, lady. [*Exits*]

GRIZEL : It's well said that woman's work is never done.

SIR G. : [*Pathetically*] I don't think I'll be giving you work much longer.

GRIZEL : Oh! Are you better then? I'm glad to hear it!

SIR G. : [*Irritated at being misunderstood*] I'm not better. I'm worse! [*Shivers violently*] Oooooh! I feel right bad, Grizel. The shivers are leaping up and down my back like salmon in the coarse waters of Tweed. And that lassie's left the door wide! [*Enter Lizzy with cloth*] Sneck it! Sneck it!

LIZZY : [*Shutting door*] Aye, Laird. [*Offers cloth to Grizel*] Here's the cloth, lady.

GRIZEL : Well, use it! Give the floor a wipe before that water gets trodden all over the place.

LIZZY : Aye, lady.

> [*Lizzy gets down on her knees and begins to wash the floor with great vigour*]

GRIZEL : [*Muttering to herself as she mends the fire*] Pottering about there, coughing and sneezing and having everybody in the house running after you! [*Aloud*] That'll do, Lizzy. I said wipe it, not wash it!

LIZZY : [*Scrambling up*] Aye, lady. [*Exits leaving the door open again*]

SIR G. : The door! Dammit, Lizzy, if I get up to you. . . .

LIZZY : [*Putting her head into room*] Aye, Sir Gideon. [*She draws door to but immediately after it is pushed open by Meg, returning with the jug of cold water*]

MEG : I brought the water straight from the well to make sure it was cold. Will I pour it in now?

SIR G. : Just a minute.

[*He tests water as before then lets both feet down into it and relaxes*]

It's gotten cold of itself.

MEG : Oh Father ! After me going out-by for it.

GRIZEL : We might have known he'd change his mind. Are you not ashamed of yourself, Gideon, causing so much trouble ?

SIR G. : I'll not be a trouble to you much longer, Grizel.

GRIZEL : You said that before. What are you hinting at, Gideon Murray ?

SIR G. : Och, it's better to say nothing about it. It would just make you feel bad. I'll bear it alone.

GRIZEL : Bear what alone ? Man, Gideon, how can a body understand you if you talk in riddles ?

MEG : Is it your belly that's hurting, Father ?

SIR G. : Well, since you mention it, it is a bit sore, but it's not that.

GRIZEL : What is it then ?

SIR G. : Maybe it would be kinder to tell you. I've had a premonition, Grizel.

GRIZEL : You've had a what ?

SIR G. : A premonition, woman ! Do you not ken what a premonition is ? I've had a premonition of my end. It came over me after dinner.

GRIZEL : That was the boiled pudding. I told you to let it pass if you'd a fever.

SIR G. : No, no, it wasn't the boiled pudding. It was a warning. The Murrays always ken when their end's near. The gift runs in the family. It was just the same with my old mother.

GRIZEL : Your mother had a premonition of her approaching end every Sabbath night regular for close on fourteen years, Gideon. You're blethering, man, blethering !

SIR G. : No, no, Grizel, you'll not talk me out of it. Eh, but I hope you'll be all right when I'm gone. I wish I had left you better provided for. It's a hard world this for two lonesome women.

GRIZEL : Gideon Murray, it's a cold in your head you've got, not your death-wound !

SIR G. : This is no ordinary cold, Grizel. I've been thinking, Grizel, after I'm gone, maybe it would be best to have Andra take over the house right away. He's not been a good son to me but he aye had a soft side for you and Meg and I'm sure he'll not grudge you a roof over your head and a bite to eat in your old age.

MEG : [*Troubled*] Mother, maybe he *is* bad ?

SIR G. : [*Angrily*] Of course I'm bad ! Am I not telling you, I'm bad as I can be !

MEG : Well, if that's so would you not be better to go to your bed like my mother's been saying ?

SIR G. : I'm not going to my bed.

GRIZEL : But what for no, Gideon ?

SIR G. : Because I don't want to go to my bed. You women are aye trying to put folk to their bed, but I'm not going to my bed and if that's all you can say to me you might as well go away through to the kitchen and leave me alone !

> [*Sir G. drags the blanket about him. Enter Lizzy. She leaves the door open then darts back and shuts it quickly as Sir G. opens his mouth to roar at her*]

LIZZY: Lady, would you come ben a minute.

GRIZEL: What's happened now?

LIZZY: I don't like the look of that pie, lady.

GRIZEL: It's not fallen in, has it?

LIZZY: No, it's not what you could call fallen: but it's got a sore dent in the waist, lady.

GRIZEL: I might have kent it with all these draughts blowing! [*Hurries to kitchen, pushing Lizzy out of her way*] Get out my feet!

[*Grizel exits, followed by Lizzy who shuts the door behind her with exaggerated caution*]

MEG: Was there anything else you wanted, Father?

SIR G.: No.

MEG: Well, if you're not wanting me I'll away through to the kitchen.

SIR G.: Oh Meg . . .

MEG: Aye?

SIR G.: Maybe if you're not doing anything more important for your mother, maybe you might bring me a wee cup of the warmed up French spirit. It slackens my cough. [*Clears his throat noisily*]

MEG: Aye, surely. Anything else, Father?

SIR G.: No, that's all.

MEG: I'll go and heat it up now.

[*Meg exits into the kitchen. Sir Gideon draws the blanket close then looking round his eye falls on a plate of scones on the table. He thinks he hears someone coming and quickly resumes his old position, but it is a false alarm and a moment later he rises cautiously, wipes his feet on a towel which was spread on his knees and tip-toes over to the table. He has taken a scone and is raising it to his*

mouth when there is a great clatter in the tower. The
tower door bursts open and Wattie, a battle-scarred
retainer, stumbles in. Sir Gideon jumps, drops the scone,
and clutches at his heart]

WATTIE : [*Excited*] Sir Gideon . . . !

SIR G. : [*Furiously*] Damn you, Wattie! How dare you
break in like that. You ken my heart's bad. The shock
might have dropped me like a stone.

WATTIE : But, Sir Gideon——

SIR G. : And you've left the door wide! Shut it, man!
Shut it! before you say another word.

[*Wattie does so*]

WATTIE : But Laird——

SIR G. : [*Returning to seat and putting his feet back in the tub*]
You'd think everybody in this house had been brought
up in a field. Well, what is it? What's put you into
such a fluster?

WATTIE : It's a THING, Sir Gideon!

SIR G. : What do you mean, a thing? What sort of a
thing?

WATTIE : I'm not right sure, Laird; but if it is, it's an
awful thing!

SIR G. : Wattie Duncan, have you been at the ale again?

WATTIE : No Laird, it's not that. It's there. I saw it as
clear as I see you.

SIR G. : Saw what? Pull yourself the-gether, man. What
did you see?

WATTIE : Well, it looked like a man and it sounded like a
man and it was the spitting image of him—but he's dead!

SIR G. : Who's dead?

WATTIE : Thomas the Rhymer.

SIR G. : Of course Thomas the Rhymer's dead. Everybody kens that. What's that got to do with us here ?

WATTIE : Just that the Thing at the door says he's him and he wants to come in, Laird.

SIR G. : [*Standing up in tub in alarm*] Good God! Did it gibber at you, Wattie ?

WATTIE : No, it just said " Good evening, Wattie! Is the Laird in ? " and " What's for supper ? "

SIR G. : It's the omen. I've been feeling this coming on all day. It's not five minutes past I was telling Grizel I had a premonition of my end.

WATTIE : What'll we do, Laird ?

SIR G. : What can we do, Wattie ? You can't hide from *them*. [*Enter Thomas by Tower door*] Oh Lord! Here it comes !

     [*Sir G. steps out of the tub and cringes away from Thomas
 —as does Wattie*]

THOMAS : [*Puzzled at this*] What's wrong ? You'd think I was a bogle from the way you're looking at me !

SIR G. : [*Tremulously*] Is it me you're seeking, Thomas ?

THOMAS : Aye! You and everybody.

WATTIE : What! Me too, Thomas ?

THOMAS : Of course. You didn't think I'd forgotten you, Wattie Duncan ? But I must say this isn't the reception I'd expected. Am I not welcome ?

SIR G. : It's such a sudden call, Thomas. 1 felt it was coming but I didn't think it would be so soon. You— you'll give me time to say a last word to Grizel and Meg, Thomas ? You'll grant me that, lad ? Just five minutes, Thomas—or ten maybe—and then I'll come with you quiet as a lamb.

23

THOMAS: [*Puzzled*] Where do you think I'm going?

SIR G.: I don't like to think on it! It's not . . . yon place, is it?

THOMAS: Yon place? What place? [*Looks from one to the other*]

WATTIE: [*Apprehensively and pointing down with a trembling hand*] . . . Y-yon place, Thomas.

[*A grin dawns on Thomas's face as he comprehends. He chuckles*]

THOMAS: So you think I'm a ghost do you?

SIR G.: What else can you be, man? [*He shrinks away as Thomas advances on him ominously*] Thomas . . . !

[*Thomas slaps him mightily on the back, sending Gideon off into a fit of coughing*]

THOMAS: There! Does that convince you I'm flesh and blood or would you like another?

SIR G.: No, that's enough. You've knocked all the puff out of me as it is. Are you not a ghost then?

THOMAS: Do I look like a ghost? I'm solid as you are. Feel that.

[*Thomas holds out his hand and Sir G. touches his arm rather gingerly*]

SIR G.: But you're dead, Thomas!

WATTIE: Aye, Thomas man. Don't you remember? You were drowned seven years past. You got roaring drunk and fell in the flood waters of Tweed. Do you not mind of it?

THOMAS: It's a libel. I never fell in the Tweed!

SIR G.: But they found your coat, man—with a scrap of ballad in the pouch of it.

THOMAS: Aye, maybe, but they didn't find me.

SIR G. : No, that's true enough. But see here, Thomas. If you're not dead, where have you been all this time?

THOMAS : I've been . . . I've been abroad, Sir Gideon.

SIR G. : In England?

THOMAS : Well, no, not just as foreign as that! If you're really interested I've been in Elfland.

SIR G. : [*Interested*] Is that so, Thomas?

THOMAS : Aye, that's so, Laird. I was enchanted.

WATTIE : Where abouts did it happen, Thomas?

THOMAS : At the bank at Huntlie. At the back of the wood yonder. You'll ken the place.

SIR G. : Well, it doesn't seem to have done you much harm. You look as hale and hearty as ever you did.

THOMAS : Oh, it's not a bad place, Elfland. But I'll tell you all about it after supper. I'm so ravenous now I couldn't do justice to it. You've not eaten yet have you?

SIR G. : No, but supper shouldn't be long. Here! Come over to the fire and make yourself at home. [*Thomas and Sir G. take seats near the fire and Sir G. begins to put on his hose and shoes*] And you, Wattie, take that tub through to the kitchen and then get up to your post. No! Wait a wee! How did you get in, Thomas?

THOMAS : I walked in. The door wasn't barred.

SIR G. : Thunder and lightning! The outside door standing wide as well? Leave that tub alone, Wattie. Get out and bar that door and then get up to your post. A fine thing it would be if we were raided and had our throats cut and it came out after that we'd neither watch set nor door shut! See to it, man! See to it!

WATTIE : [*Slouching out without haste*] Ach, there's not much chance of anybody raiding us in these peely-wally days.

> [*Wattie exits grumbling by the tower door, and Meg enters from kitchen carrying a glass of steaming brandy. The glass is so full that she has to keep her eyes on it to avoid spilling the liquor so she does not see Thomas*]

MEG : Here's the glass of the French spirit you wanted. I'm sorry I've been so long.

> [*Before Sir Gideon can take it Thomas rises, intercepts the glass, and drinks it off at a draught*]

THOMAS : Thank you, lass. That was well thought of.

MEG : [*Blinking at him*] That was for my father!

THOMAS : Was it?

SIR G. : It was!

THOMAS : Oh well, it wasn't wasted. Here's the glass, lass. Hallo? What's taken you? Why are you looking at me like that? [*To her*] You're not Meg, are you? I believe you *are* Meg!

MEG : I'm Meg all right, but who are you?

SIR G. : Don't you remember him, Meg?

MEG : He's the living image of Thomas the Rhymer that came about Elibank in the old days. But Thomas is dead! He was drowned!

THOMAS : Do I look as if I was drowned?

MEG : Everybody said you were drowned. They found your coat in the Tweed.

THOMAS : Folk are too quick at jumping to conclusions in these parts. I was never drowned in my life. [*Looking her up and down*] My! but you've grown. You're a right lady that were all legs and braids and mouth when I saw you last.

MEG : [*A little put out*] You needn't have mentioned the mouth, Thomas. Och, but you didn't mean any harm and I'm right glad you're not drowned. [*Going towards kitchen door*] Mother ! Come ben the now. Thomas the Rhymer's back.

GRIZEL : [*Off*] What !

    [*Enter Grizel*]

Guidsakes, it's him right enough ! [*To others*] I told you he'd never drown.

THOMAS : Thank you, Lady Grizel. I'm glad somebody at Elibank had the wit to ken it would take more than a bucket of water to give Thomas the Rhymer his quietus.

SIR G. : It was Grizel's opinion you would end on the gallows or not at all.

THOMAS : Och, Lady Grizel !

GRIZEL : Aye, and I still hold to my view. But stand back and let's have a look at you. My, but you're braw, aren't you ? [*To him and fingering his doublet*] That's as fine a bit of velvet as I've ever set fingers on. Feel that, Meg.

MEG : Oh, isn't it soft !

GRIZEL : [*Feeling Thomas's hose*] And will you look at his hose ! Real silk ! I've never seen the like of it.

THOMAS : [*Retreating*] Here, that's enough ! You're tickling.

GRIZEL : Where on earth did you get them, Thomas ? I haven't seen braws like that since the Spanish ship was wrecked at St. Abb's. Have you been robbing somebody?

MEG : Mother, that's not a nice-like thing to say to a body.

GRIZEL : Ach ! Thomas and me understand each other fine. Come on, Thomas. Out with it ! Where did you get them ?

THOMAS : They were gifted, lady . . .

GRIZEL : Oh, and who by ?

THOMAS : The Queen of Elfland herself, lady.

GRIZEL : [*With laugh*] That for a story ! It's likely the Queen of Elfland would take up with a body like you with the whole world to draw on for company.

THOMAS : Well, believe it or not, it's the God's truth, lady. I've been in Elfland for seven years and I'll give you the whole tale of it the night after supper. By the by, you're surely eating awful late the night ?

GRIZEL : We're all behind on account of Gideon. But it shouldn't be long now. Away through, Meg, and see what that limmer Lizzy's doing. And watch that pie !

MEG : But Mother, I want to hear about Elfland.

THOMAS : Go and watch that pie, lass : my mouth's fair watering for it. I promise you I'll not say one word about Elfland until you're back.

MEG : All right, Thomas. [*To door*] And I'm right glad you're not drowned.

THOMAS : So am I, Meg. So am I. [*Meg exits*] My, but she's changed. She's a grown woman now that was just a prattling bairn when I was here last.

GRIZEL : We're all changed, Thomas, except yourself. You ken you don't look a day older than when last we saw you ?

THOMAS : Time goes at a queer rate in Elfland, lady. But you're looking well, yourself, for that matter.

GRIZEL : I'm fifty-two, Thomas.

THOMAS : I'd never have believed it ! And you, Sir Gideon, how's all with you these days ?

SIR G. : Oh, bad, bad. I'm breaking up I fear.

THOMAS: I'm sorry to hear it. What's gone wrong with you?

GRIZEL: He's got a cold in the head.

THOMAS: Oh, is that why you'd your legs in that tub of water, when I came in?

SIR G.: Why else would I have my legs in a tub of water?

THOMAS: I thought you were washing your feet.

SIR G.: Away with you, man!

GRIZEL: Do you think Meg's changed a lot, Thomas? In features I mean?

THOMAS: I would hardly have kent her.

GRIZEL: She's two and twenty.

THOMAS: Is she that? Dear me, it seems no time at all since she was pulling at my whiskers and saying baw-baw. And she's not wed yet?

GRIZEL: No, Thomas. She's not wed yet.

THOMAS: She'll be betrothed though?

GRIZEL: [*With sigh*] There's not a hint of it, Thomas.

THOMAS: Umm, and she's two and twenty! Aye, it's a pity for her. She's a good lass, but two and twenty! It's a sore age in a woman, Lady Grizel.

GRIZEL: I ken. It's a fearful thought but I'm beginning to fear she'll be left on our hands. Poor lassie. Poor lassie.

THOMAS: What went wrong exactly? I should have thought you'd have had no trouble in marrying her off. With just the one son well settled you can afford to give her a good dowrie.

SIR G.: It's her mouth, Thomas. I don't know if you noticed it but her mou's on the muckle side.

GRIZEL: It's not her mouth at all. Her mouth's not much

bigger than mine and I had plenty of men after me. No,
it's all the fault of a silly rhyme.

THOMAS : Oh ?

GRIZEL : I wouldn't sully my lips by repeating it.

SIR G. : I think I mind how it goes. Something like this,
Thomas :

" Meg of Elibank had a mou'
    Where you could stall a Galloway coo,
    And if her teeth were drawn aside
    The herd as well could bide inside ! "

[*Trying not to laugh*] That's the sense of it anyway.

GRIZEL : I just wish I could get my hands on the gomeril
that made it : I'd clatter his lugs for him ! Thomas !
It wasn't you ?

    [*Thomas is very embarrassed*]

THOMAS : Well, now you mention it, I believe it was.

GRIZEL : [*Rising*] Thomas !

THOMAS : [*Rising*] I meant no harm, Lady. She was only
a bairn then.

GRIZEL : Well, you should be black-ashamed of yourself.
That rhyme's gone all over the countryside and now
nobody can look at her without the sound of it jingling
in their ears. It's ruined the lassie's life.

THOMAS : I'm right sorry, Lady. It's such a bad rhyme,
too. It can do no manner of good to my reputation.

GRIZEL : Your reputation ! Is that what you're thinking
of ? And what about the harm it's done Meg's reputation ?

THOMAS : [*Impatiently*] Well, I've said I'm sorry, haven't

30

I? But wait a wee! If I mind right there was some sort of understanding that Meg was to marry the young Laird of Dalkeith?

GRIZEL: Yon billie! Don't mention his name to me.

THOMAS: Why, what went wrong there?

SIR G.: He went back on his father's word, Thomas. He wouldn't have her. I did everything possible but it was no good. I even offered to throw in the wee black bull with the dowrie, but he just laughed at me. Laughed at me!

GRIZEL: He had the audacity to send word that if we'd half Meg's mouth and double the dowrie he'd think on it, but not otherwise.

THOMAS: [*Jumping up, his hand on his dirk*] Man, Laird, but you'll not stand for that? Fighting was never my game but if it's strength that you lack for it, give me a dozen men and I'll ride to Dalkeith the night and ram these words down his throat with the head of a pike! [*Shouting*] Hi! Wattie! Jock!

SIR G.: [*Calming him*] Wheest man, wheest! Your feelings do you credit but you don't know what you're saying.

[*Enter Wattie, sword in hand*]

WATTIE: What's the steer?

[*Enter Jock clutching firelock*]

JOCK: What's up?

SIR G.: [*Waving them off*] It's all right. You're not wanted. [*Wattie and Jock exit looking perplexed*] Man, Thomas, do you not ken me better than that? If it had been possible I'd have been at Dalkeith long ago. But it's not possible. Things are very different on the border from what they were seven years past. The days of the pike are done,

Thomas. When we get an insult nowadays we must gulp it down with what grace we can—and wait for a chance to put matters right with a dirk on a moonless night. There's no other way.

THOMAS : It's not a way that I like much.

SIR G. : Nor me, Thomas, nor me ! But that's the way that things are now and we must just put up with it. The good days are done, Thomas. They're done, man ! Do you ken this ? Everything's that centred now with the King in Edinburgh that a man can't hang one of his own tenants on his own gallows without some birkie from the court poking his nose in and asking awkward questions !

THOMAS : You'll be telling me there's no fighting next !

SIR G. : And there isn't, Thomas ! There's not been a broil on the border for two years. Not one, Thomas !

GRIZEL : And that's the one good change that we have seen. I've no more liking than Gideon for a deal of the changes we've seen lately but I was never sorry to see the end of the fighting. Fighting's all right for the men, but it's naught but work and worry for the women, and always was.

THOMAS : But what in the world do you do with yourselves? How do you put in your time ?

SIR G. : We just farm the lands, Thomas, look after the beasts and raise the crops.

THOMAS : It sounds awful dull.

[*Enter Wattie*]

SIR G. : Now what is it ?

WATTIE : [*Seating himself*] I've been relieved. [*Looking at table*] What's happened to supper the night ?

32

GRIZEL : It's just coming.

SIR G. : It is late.

GRIZEL : I thought you'd no appetite ?

SIR G. : You don't want me to give up altogether, do you ?

GRIZEL : [*Rising*] All right, all right. I'll away and hurry
it on. You men are always thinking about your meat.
If you had the making of it you wouldn't be so gluttonous.
[*Exits into kitchen banging the door*]

SIR G. : Who's watching now, Wattie ?

WATTIE : Jock. Not that it makes any odds. Since Lady
Grizel raised the two new bedchambers on the west
battlement you can't see farther than the gate from
up there. If we were raided—and that's not likely !—
they'd be in on top of us before the guard could cry
" Shote ! "

SIR G. : That's not the point, Wattie. As I've told you
before, this is a border keep and a border keep must be
watched. Besides, what's the good of having a watch-
tower if you don't use it ?

WATTIE : What's the use of having a watchman if he can't
see ?

SIR G. : [*Rising in sorrow and anger*] Wattie Duncan, will
you stop your argie-bargying ? If I say there'll be a
watchman there'll be a watchman and that's the end
of it !

WATTIE : All right ! All right !

SIR G. : [*Beginning quietly but his voice rising as his ire mounts*]
The trouble with you, Wattie, is that you keep forgetting
the difference between us. The fact that you're a twenty-
seventh cousin of Grizel's and that you saved me from
a bit of jag in yon brush with the Scotts at the Black

Burn, doesn't alter the other fact that I'm Sir Gideon
Murray and that you're nothing but a blethering old
cheat-the-gallows o' a kye lifter! Do you hear me?

WATTIE: Aye, I hear you. I'm not deaf!

SIR G.: Well, mind what I'm telling you.

THOMAS: [*Dreamily*] Yon was a grand fight, yon.

SIR G.: Eh? What was that, Thomas?

THOMAS: I was saying yon was a grand fight. The one
at the Black Burn.

SIR G.: [*Softening*] Aye, so it was. I often think back on
it. You were there weren't you?

THOMAS: Aye, I watched it.

SIR G.: [*With chuckle*] Dod! I can't help laughing even
now, when I remember the look on old Baldie's face
when I caught him by the heel, after he'd unhorsed me,
and tumbled him head first into the burn!

WATTIE: [*Rising and acting it out*] And Rod Lindsay,
Gideon. Do you mind how I jouked under the pike
and whacked him over the head with the broken spear-
shaft? Man! Yon were the days. Yon were the days!

SIR G.: [*With happy sigh*] Aye, Wattie, you're right, you're
right. [*Becoming respectable*] Not but what the country was
fearful unlawsome mind!

WATTIE: I ken, Laird. Everybody seemed to do just
whatever they wanted then. Life was just a round of
pleasure.

SIR G.: That's true, Wattie. We were no more civilized
than the beasts of the field and the heathen savages
in the wilds of Fife, but say what you will there
was a sort of lightsomeness in the air then that's gone
now. You must have noticed that, Thomas?

34

THOMAS: Well, I've not rightly had time yet. I'm just back you see.

WATTIE: Oh there's no doubt of it, Thomas! Why, man, the world even smells different! I can mind mornings riding home behind a herd of Cumberland kye when the wind had a top to it like a jug of the fresh-drawn ale— one sniff set you singing!

SIR G.: He's right, Thomas. And here's a queer thing. The flowers aren't half so bonny as they used to be.

THOMAS: Are you saying?

SIR G.: No, they're not a patch on what they were even seven years back—and as for fifty. . . . Man, when I was a lad just put on metal there was such a glory in a bush of the wild rose blooming that a man had to slash at it quick before he burst out weeping and shamed his manhood.

WATTIE: Aye, and even the common things are not what they were now. There was taste to a bannock then. Oatmeal wasn't the wersh stuff that they serve you now. As for the ale! The secret's lost, man. Lost! There's not such a drink any more. It's just yellow water, yellow water.

THOMAS: And the folk, are they changed too?

SIR G.: Changed? They hardly merit the name of folk any more. They'd make you spew the most of them. You'll be sorely disappointed in the lassies, Thomas.

THOMAS: Oh?

SIR G.: Aye! Do you mind yon bonny glow you'd see on a young thing's face when she turned to look up at you?

THOMAS: I know what you mean.

35

SIR G. : Well, it's gone. I haven't seen yon look on the face of a lass for years and years. They're all hard as stones now—hearts and faces!

THOMAS : And all this has been happening while I was away?

SIR G. : That's right, Thomas. Once you start progressing there's no stopping it.

THOMAS : It begins to look as if the Queen of Elfland was right. This is no world for a poet. I've half a mind to go straight back.

SIR G. : I wouldn't blame you if you did. [*Listening*] That's not a horse, Wattie?

    [*Wattie listens*]

WATTIE : [*Rising*] It is, Laird, and whoever's on it's fair licking on.

    [*The horseman is heard riding up at a gallop and reining in sharply*]

RAB : [*Off*] Wo there! Hi! Open up, will you? I want Sir Gideon.

WATCHMAN : [*Off*] Who's there? Speak up, or I'll blow your head off!

RAB : [*Off*] If you do, Jock, you'll be sorry after. Come on! Open the door and let's in. It's me—Rab Wilson.

SIR G. : It's drunken Rab. What the de'il's brought him up to Elibank so late? [*To Thomas*] He's living down in the town now—in his sister's house.

THOMAS : It must be an ale-house if Rab Wilson stays in it long. Or is he changed too?

SIR G. : Not in that particular.

    [*Enter Jock, cap-à-pie and carrying his old firelock. He*

is followed by Rab, a thin little man with a glassy eye.
Rab is in his usual state of semi-intoxication]

JOCK : Here's Droucken Rab wanting you, Sir Gideon.
He says he's got a message for you.

RAB : [*Swaying*] O' the greatest importance !

SIR G. : [*To him*] Well, what is it, Rab ? What's brought
you up in such a flurry ? Sit down, man. Sit down.

[*Sir G. places a chair and seats Rab in it, then steps*
back. Rab shuts his eyes, straightens himself and opening
his eyes announces with drunken gravity——]

RAB : Sir Gideon, you're going to be raided !

WATTIE : [*Joyously*] The Lord be thanked ! When, Rab ?
When ?

SIR G. : Man, you're daft. There hasn't been a raid in
these parts for eight years.

RAB : I don't give a button. There'll be one the night or
Dick Scott's a liar as well as a drunken tyke. " We'll
raid Elibank," said he. " We'll pick Elibank cleaner of
meat than a flock o' corbies can pick a bone in a twelvemonth. We'll get our own back for the fray at the
burn," he said. He was drunk, Sir Gideon. Roaring !
I was fair disgusted with him. It's an awful thing,
drink !

[*Rab's head falls forward on his chest and he drops off*
asleep. Sir G. and Wattie grab him and shake him
roughly]

SIR G. : Here, Rab ! Waken up ! Waken up ! You can't
fall asleep now. Where did you hear all this ?

RAB : Eh ?

SIR G. : I said, where did you hear this ?

RAB : In the Reiver's Arms, Sir Gideon. Yesterday night.

SIR G. : Yesterday night?

RAB : That's what I said. Yesterday night.

SIR G. : But hell's cinders, man, if you're speaking true they'll be here any minute! What did you not come up before for you drunken wastrel!

RAB : I meant to, Sir Gideon. I did mean to, but to tell you the truth, Laird, I was gye fu' myself. [*Slumps down in chair*]

SIR G. : Were you ever anything else? But there's no time for talk. Grizel! [*To Wattie and Jock*] Here you. Take this out and throw a bucket of water over it. We'll need every man we can get. Get yourself metalled and the horses out.

WATTIE : JOCK : [*Together*] Aye, Laird.

  [*They hurry out dragging Rab with them. Grizel and Meg run in*]

GRIZEL : What's happened, Gideon?

MEG : Is your cold worse, Father?

SIR G. : [*Taking corselet from wall and donning it*] Cold? What cold? I've no time for colds. Help me on with this corselet, Grizel! Get my sword, Meg. Hurry! Don't stand there gaping.

  [*Meg runs and brings sword from wall*]

GRIZEL : [*Fastening corselet*] Is it a raid, Gideon?

SIR G. : Aye, the Scotts. They're on their way now Rab Wilson says. [*To Meg who is trying to buckle his sword on*] Not that side! Good God! Do you not ken how to belt on a sword yet? Let's see it myself. [*To Thomas*] You'll look after the women, Thomas?

THOMAS : Leave them to me, Laird.

  [*There is a clatter of hooves outside and Wattie, cap-*]

à-pie, leather-jerkined and with a pike in his hand runs in]

WATTIE : The horses are outby, Laird !

SIR G. : I'm coming ! [*Wattie exits*] [*To Thomas, Grizel and Meg*] Keep the door barred and don't open it unless you're sure it's us. And keep that window fast.

GRIZEL : [*Running up to him with a red scarf which she flings round his neck*] Here ! Put this on.

SIR G. : [*Trying to push her off unsuccessfully*] Woman ! How can I fight with a thing like that on ?

GRIZEL : You keep it on, Gideon. I've had enough trouble with the one cold without your getting another on top of it.

[*Enter Wattie*]

WATTIE : Are you coming ?

SIR G. : Aye. I'm coming !

[*He exits after Wattie, banging the door*]

GRIZEL : So it's started again. 1 was afraid the good days wouldn't last.

MEG : What does it all mean ?

THOMAS : [*Happily*] It means that things aren't so different on the border as your father and Wattie were trying to tell me a while back.

GRIZEL : Wheest !

SIR G. : [*Off*] Come on, lads. On your way !

[*We hear the horses galloping off. With turning heads Meg, Grizel and Thomas follow their departure*]

ACT II

SCENE ONE

The hall at Elibank twenty minutes later. At the table which has been drawn to one side, Grizel and Meg are busily engaged making bandages. Thomas, standing on a stool under a shuttered window, listening for the start of the battle. Lizzy is pouring water into the pot.

LIZZY : Will that do, lady ?

GRIZEL : Is it full ?

LIZZY : [*Considering*] It's near to full.

GRIZEL : Near to full'll not do. Fill it right up.

> [*Lizzy exits sighing for another jugful. Meg stops work and looks at the heap of bandages on the table*]

MEG : You're surely expecting a deal of them to be hurt, Mother ?

GRIZEL : [*Briskly*] It's better to be prepared. I'll be sore disappointed if they're not needed ! The cheek of the Scotts—to come raiding us with the whole of Northumbria to go gallivanting about in !

MEG : I wasn't thinking about the Scotts, Mother. I was thinking about Father, and Wattie and the other Elibank lads.

GRIZEL : Huh ! You needn't worry about your father. If ever I kent a man able to look after himself it's your father.

MEG: You're awful hard, Mother. He's not as young as he used to be.

GRIZEL: No, but he's twice as cunning to make up for it. Just you get on with your work, and don't fret yourself about the men. They're enjoying themselves fine. [*With feeling*] You can save your pity for the women in times like these!

MEG: Indeed and it is an awful thing to see the brave lads riding out into the big dark of the shadow of death and ken they may never return.

GRIZEL: [*Straightening herself*] Meg Murray, will you stop talking downright nonsense? What do you think this is—the battle of Flodden? I wouldn't wonder if the brave lads weren't a lot safer out there than in a Selkirk tavern on a Fair night. It wasn't that that my mind was running on when I said you should save your pity for us. No! nor anything like it!

MEG: No?

GRIZEL: No! It was the fine dirty mess that they'll be getting their clothes into and all the washing, and sewing and mending that I'll be let in for the morn while they sit about there eating and drinking and lying and boasting and deafening everybody that'll listen to them with tales of their marvellous exploits! Fighting? Huh! I ken all about fighting!

THOMAS: [*Looking round with frown*] Wheest! will you.

GRIZEL: [*Bristling*] No, I'll not wheest!

MEG: Did you hear something, Thomas?

THOMAS: How can I hear anything with your mother and you yattering away there like broody hens! Be quiet for a minute, will you? [*Listening, ear close to shutter*]

41

No, I can't hear it now. See ! Come up beside me, Meg.
Maybe your ears are sharper.

MEG : [*Climbing up on stool*] Hold me tight now.

THOMAS : I've got you. [*A pause*] Well, do you hear
anything ?

MEG : What am I supposed to hear ?

THOMAS : Horses.

      [*Meg listens intently*]

MEG : It's awful still. There's a hoolit crying somewhere
and I can hear the rush of the burn. [*Turning round to
Grizel*] That's queer, Mother. I never kent you could
hear the burn from the house. . . .

THOMAS : [*Jerking her back to the shutter*] Never mind the
burn. You can listen to the burn the morn. Can you
hear anything else ?

MEG : No. [*Hears something*] eh ?

THOMAS : There ! I told you ! That was scree slipping
under a hoof or I'm an Englishman. They're here, Meg.
They're here ! [*A bull is heard bellowing*] That's the wee
black bull roaring. He aye kens when there's trouble
brewing.

MEG : Might it not be my father we heard ?

THOMAS : The Laird ? No—he's not so daft ! He'll be
sitting tight, hardly breathing, waiting his time to bang
at them when they least expect it.

GRIZEL : Aye, but where ? I hope he's not dropped
off to sleep on his way to the pound. It would be a
fine thing if the Scotts drove off the beasts under his
nose.

THOMAS : If I mind the lie of the land, he and the Elibank
lads'll be up in the fir clump yonder waiting till the

Scotts are packed in the narrow cut at the gate of the pound. Then when he drops on them they'll have no room to use their pikes. But listen!

SIR G. : [*Shouting in distance*] Right lads! Let them have it!
    [*There is a cheer and clatter of hooves then the confused noises of battle filter into the hall*]

THOMAS : They're off! Now we'll hear something!
[*Shouting*] Go on the Scotts! Caw the heads off them! God's blood I wish I could see! [*He begins to open the shutters but Grizel hurries up and clashes them to*]

GRIZEL : Leave the shutters alone, Thomas!
    [*Meg jumps down from the stool and puts her hands to her ears. Outside the din of battle mounts—the clash of arms : the thud of hooves : the cries of the combatants : " Murray! Murray! " " Scotts here! " " At 'em lads," etc.*]

MEG : [*Running to Grizel in dismay*] Oh, Mother! They'll all be killed!

GRIZEL : Don't you believe it, hinny. In half an hour you'll be wondering what they were making all the noise about. [*She puts her arm round Meg*]
    [*Enter Lizzy with jug. She stands gaping*]

LIZZY : My! They're fair going their dingers down there. I hope my Jock's looking after himself. I wouldn't like him to get a dunt.

GRIZEL : [*To her and giving her a push*] Well, standing there'll not help him. Go on. Put that water in the pot and get out the ale cups.
    [*Lizzy pours water into pot, fiddles with fire and then exits slowly with backward glances*]

MEG : I don't know how you can think of ale cups with

43

my father maybe lying out there under the hooves of the horses, swimming in gore.

GRIZEL : [*Back at table*] Rubbish ! Here, hold this. [*Thrusts end of long strip of cloth into Meg's hand*] And keep your thumb out of the way or I'll crop it. [*She deliberately jags Meg with the scissors to take her attention from the battle*]

MEG : Oh ! You jagged me !

[*Meg puts her thumb in her mouth*]

GRIZEL : It serves you right. You should keep your mind on your work.

[*The battle noises swell up again*]

THOMAS : Losh ! They're putting up a grand fight down there. I thought the Scotts would have cut and run at the first onset, but there must be a great gang of them. It's more than bicker ; its a battle ! [*He jumps down from stool*] By the Queen of Elfland ! There's my ballad. [*Quieter*] Let me see now. [*He begins to walk up and down muttering*] Elibank, bank, lank, hank, dank, lank . . . lank ! When the grass grows green and lank !

GRIZEL : Have you gone daft, Thomas ?

THOMAS : Wheest, woman ! I'm inspired ! I've started a ballad. [*Puts his foot on a stool and recites*]

" It fell about the Lammastide
    When the grass grows green and lank
    The Harden Scotts they swore an oath
    That they'd reive Elibank."

GRIZEL : [*Coldly*] It's not Lammas.

THOMAS : [*Coming to*] What's that ?

44

GRIZEL: I said it's not Lammas.

THOMAS: What the de'il's that to do with it? This is a
work of art; not an almanack!

> [*The harp of Elfland recalling his wager with the Elfland
> Queen sounds. Only Thomas hears it. He cringes*]

Oh losh! But you're right though! I forgot. Ach, to
hell! I'll sort it later. Now, where was I? Oh aye,
I've got it. [*To Grizel*] Don't interrupt me again. It puts
me right off my beat. [*Recites*]

" They mounted on their good fleet steeds
    And blyth of heart were they,
    Nor recked they o' the widow's weeds
    Would spout afore the day.

" Aye, little thought they as they rode
    Under the golden moon
    That Sir Gideon Murray had gathered his men
        and was——"

MEG: [*Indignantly*] Oh, stop it, Thomas, stop it!

THOMAS: Are you speaking to me?

MEG: You should be black-ashamed at yourself making
up silly rhymes at a time like this!

THOMAS: Lassie, are you aware that I'm creating a body
of work that'll be the admiration and envy of later
generations?

MEG: If you were half a man you would be down there
helping my father!

THOMAS: [*Amused and very patient*] Lassie, you don't understand. It's all right for folk like your father and Wattie
to dive head-first into every bicker that comes their way.

They've got nothing better to do. But I can't afford to take risks like that. If anything happened to me who'd write the ballad of the battle?

MEG: How can you make the ballad of a battle you've never seen?

THOMAS: I've got my imagination, haven't I?

MEG: Aye, but where's your facts?

THOMAS: Facts! Facts would just hamper me. Facts are of no manner of use to a poet, Meg. What a poet needs is vision! Vision!

GRIZEL: Seems they're about done out there.

[*The battle noises fade into distance*]

THOMAS: I believe you're right. Aye, here's some of them now.

[*A horse is heard galloping up and there is a loud knocking at the door*]

SIR G.: [*Off*] Open up! Open up, Grizel! It's me. We've won!

GRIZEL: It's Gideon! [*Hurrying to outer door*] I'm coming. You needn't knock the door down. [*Hastily: Off*] Are you all right?

[*Lizzy enters with ale cups and taking ale jug from corner fills them hastily*]

SIR G.: Champion! Grizel. Champion! [*He enters followed by Grizel*] Man Thomas, you missed yourself! It was better than the Black Burn. We knocked hell out of their hides and they're riding for Harden like scalded cats with our lads on their tails harrying them. I wouldn't have missed it for worlds! [*To Grizel*] Is there no ale in the house?

GRIZEL: Get the ale, Meg.

MEG: [*Taking cup from table and passing it to her father*] Here you are, Father.

THOMAS: Did you come down on them from behind the firs, when they were in the gulley, Laird?

[*Sir G. swallows the ale at a draught*]

SIR G.: That's right, Thomas. That was the plan. We kept quiet up there till they were all herded close in the narrow place with no room for their pikes, then down dropped on them like a tumbled cairn. Man! I'll wager they're still wondering what hit them! Is there no more ale?

MEG: [*Who has a second cup in hand ready, supplies him*] Here you are, Father.

GRIZEL: Where's the rest of the Elibank lads, Gideon?

SIR G.: Harrying them on I told you. All except Wattie and Jock. [*He drinks*]

GRIZEL: What's the matter with Wattie and Jock?

MEG: They're not hurt, are they?

SIR G.: Hurt? No! They're bringing up the prisoner.

GRIZEL: Oh, you caught one of them, did you? Who is he, Gideon?

SIR G.: God kens yet. It's black as the underside of a peat moss down there and *he* was in no condition to say. He's a big strapping lad though.

THOMAS: [*Snapping his fingers*] I'll work him into the ballad. It's just what it needs for development.

MEG: Father, what'll you do with the prisoner?

SIR G.: Hang him!

THOMAS: [*Pleasantly*] It's customary.

MEG: I suppose he deserves it.

47

SIR G. : Deserves it? I'll say he deserves it! I just wish
I'd three more to hang alongside him.

GRIZEL : Is he badly hurt, Gideon?

SIR G. : Not from the noise he was making before Wattie
tapped him on the head with his pistol. But we'll soon
see. [*To door and opening it*] Hi, there! Wattie! Jock!
What the devil are you playing at? If you've let that
thieving cateran escape I'll hang you by the heels in the
hall chimney!

WATTIE : [*Off*] We're coming. We're coming.

THOMAS : [*Going*] I'll give them a hand with him, Laird.

SIR G. : Aye, do, Thomas.

> [*Sir Gideon takes off his corselet and rubs himself under
> the arms*]

That's better! I'll have to have something done about
this corselet, Grizel. It grips me below the oxsters.

MEG : [*Near door*] Here they come.

SIR G. : Bring him in, Wattie. Bring him in.

> [*Enter Wattie, Thomas and Jock carrying the prisoner.
> A stalwart young man whose face is masked by mud and
> blood*]

WATTIE : Where'll we drop him?

SIR G. : There, man, there! Put him in the chair.

> [*The bearers dump the prisoner in the chair and straighten
> themselves, wiping their brows*]

MEG : Oh, you've hurt him! His face is all blood!

GRIZEL : [*Drawing her back*] Come here, Meg.

SIR G. : [*Surveying the prisoner*] He's a Scott all right. But
which Scott?

WATTIE : [*Surveying him*] He's not Rab Scott and he's not
Alex Scott.

SIR G. : I didn't ask who he wasn't. I asked who he was.
Here, you, Thomas, you've been up at that thieves' den
at Harden many a time. Do you ken him ?

THOMAS : His face is that mucky he might be any of them.
See Lizzy, take a cloth and give him a wipe.

LIZZY : Me ? I wouldn't touch the murdering blackguard !

GRIZEL : Oh, you wouldn't ! Wouldn't you ? Then just
you take yourself off if you can't make yourself useful.
Away through and clean up the kitchen ! Go on now !
[*Lizzy exits*]

MEG : [*With above*] I'll do it, Thomas. [*She takes one of the
bandages and wipes Willie's face*] Oh, the poor lad. That's
a right sore dunt he's had on his brow.

SIR G. : He'll get a sorer dunt on his neck the morn. Out
the way, Meg ! There's no call to cuddle him. Wattie,
is he not Willie Scott ?
[*Wattie lifts the prisoner's head by his forelock and turns
it this way and that*]

WATTIE : Man, Laird, I believe you're right ! Aye ! Look !
There's the nick on the ear he got in the fight with
Jimmy Marshall. Losh ! We've caught the Cock o' the
Border !
[*Wattie slaps Sir G. on the shoulder and turns to shake
hands with Jock*]

SIR G. : Well, well, he'll not crow so proud in a tow
collar !
[*He takes the prisoner by the shoulders and shakes him
roughly*] Hi ! Waken up, Willie ! Waken up !

MEG : Father, you'll hurt him !

SIR G. : Aye, I'll hurt him ! [*He shakes him again*] Ah, he's
coming to now.

[*Willie groans and opens his eyes: staggers to his feet: shuts his eyes, sways, and blinks about him, holding a hand to his brow*]

WILLIE : Oh my head ! Where am I ?

SIR G. : So you're not dead, Willie ?

[*Willie, dazed, peers at him*]

WILLIE : What hit me ?

WATTIE : [*Coming forward*] I hit you.

WILLIE : [*Looking round*] This . . . this isn't Elibank, is it ?

SIR G. : Man, you're bright, aren't you ?

WILLIE : What are you going to do with me, Murray ?

SIR G. : Hang you, Willie. Hang you !

WILLIE : You don't mean it ?

SIR G. : Of course I mean it ! You'll hang the morn, Willie, and I wish I'd three more to hang beside you. I said I'd do it and I will.

WILLIE : My father'll not like this, Murray.

SIR G. : I'm not doing it to please your father. Take him away, Wattie. Put him down in the dungeon.

WATTIE : Aye, aye, Laird. Come on, Willie. First on the left and straight down. [*He takes Willie's arm*]

WILLIE : [*Shaking him off*] Wait a bit. Listen, Murray, I warn you if you go on with this the red cock'll crow on the rafters of Elibank before the year's out.

SIR G. : Take him away, Wattie ! I'm weary listening to him.

WATTIE : Will you come quiet, Willie, or do you want a crack on the other side ? [*Threatens him with his pistol butt*]

WILLIE : I'll come when I'm ready ! One word more, Murray.

SIR G. : Well, what is it ?

WILLIE : Just this, Murray. [*His voice rising to a shout*] Don't you think that you'll ever get the better of the Scotts ! Maybe you came out top in the fight the night, but let me tell you this, if I wasn't so shoogly on my legs and so peely-wally in the arms, I'd take on the whole clanjamphry of you here and now and knock the stuffing out of you with my——

SIR G. : [*During above*] Away with him !

[*Wattie hits Willie on the head with his pistol and Willie slumps in the retainer's arms*]

WATTIE : [*Reproachfully*] I'm surprised at you, Willie.

[*Wattie and Jock exit dragging Willie with them, his heels trailing*]

MEG : [*Suddenly*] What a braw young man ! [*To Sir Gideon*] You're not serious about hanging him, Father ?

SIR G. : Of course I'm serious ! Did you think I was joking ?

MEG : It seems an awful waste with braw lads so scarce !

SIR G. : Well, here's a new change to the tune. If I mind right you were saying yourself before we brought him in, he deserved hanging !

MEG : Aye, but I hadn't seen him then. [*Her hand flies to her mouth when she realises what she has said*]

SIR G. : Oh ! so that's the airt that the wind's in ! Now tell me, what would you like me to do with the young birkie ? Turn him loose with my regrets that he didn't get off with our cattle, and with my best wishes for a better outcome on a future occasion ? Lassie ! what do you want ?

MEG : Could you not give him to me, Father ?

SIR G.: Give him to you? You're daft, Meg!

GRIZEL: [*Suddenly*] No, she's not! Meg, you've got more sense in your wee finger than there is in the rest of the Murrays put together. That's just what you must do, Gideon. You must give him to Meg.

SIR G.: Have you gone off your head too? What do you think Willie Scott is?—a wee dog to make a plaything of? He's a reiver, woman—a lawless stick-at-nothing cattle thief. You can't make a play-doll of the likes of him!

GRIZEL: You're not wise, Gideon. I meant *marry* the pair of them. Give Willie Scott the option of marrying Meg or of being hung.

THOMAS: [*Reasonably*] It's original. There's no doubt that it's original. But it'll not do! There's no pathos in such an end, and you've got to have pathos in a ballad. Don't you listen to her, Laird.

GRIZEL: You keep out of this, Thomas. When we want your opinion we'll ask for it. Well, Gideon, what do you say?

SIR G.: I'm so flabbergasted I can hardly say anything. Marry a Harden Scott to an Elibank Murray? Marry a land-roving, thieving, ne'er-do-well to my own born daughter? Do you know what you're saying, woman?

GRIZEL: She's got to marry somebody, Gideon.

MEG: If I don't mind I don't see that you should, Father.

SIR G.: Thomas, did I only dream that a band of blood-thirsty de'ils made a raid on my herds the night?

GRIZEL: [*With impatient gesture*] Good God! man. You wouldn't hold that against Willie? This would be but

a desert airt of the border if every man here that's lifted
a stirk had to face the gallows ! Aye, and I wouldn't feel
over comfortable about yourself, Gideon, were such a
state of affairs to arise !

MEG : Oh ! Did you go out reiving too, Father ?

SIR G. : [*Embarrassed*] Ach, that was a long time ago, Meg.
Besides it was quite different. I took beasts from the
English.

MEG : We're not far from the border, father. Maybe the
Scotts made a mistake the night.

SIR G. : [*With guffaw*] Aye, certes, they did ! Certes, they
did !

GRIZEL : Don't try to be sarcastic, Gideon. You haven't
the head for it. Now, just calm down, listen to me, and
try to see a bit farther than the end of your nose.
The plain facts of the matter are these. If you hang
Willie Scott, we'll have nothing but trouble, trouble,
trouble till the end of our days. The Harden Scotts are
not the kind to keep quiet under a slight of that kind—
as well you ken—and they'll take it sore ill-out if they
hear that their darling Willie's been danced a rope jig
on the Elibank battlements ! Go on with this, Gideon,
and there'll be no more sitting about the fire for you of
a winter night with your boots off. Oh no, Gideon.
Hang Willie and you'll eat in harness, you'll sleep in
harness aye, and one black night, sooner or later, you'll
die in harness ! It's the truth, Gideon.

SIR G. : [*Blustering*] I'm not afraid of the Scotts ! I've
beat them before. I'll beat them again ! Let them all
come !

GRIZEL : That's bairn's talk ! Listen now. You're not

going to tell me you *want* to spend the rest of your days
in a storm of tulzies ?

SIR G. : Well, maybe not. But all the same——

GRIZEL : Then don't you see that this is a chance in a
thousand ? With the one stroke you can give Meg
her man and put an end to the bad blood between
the families. Why Gideon ! If the Scotts and the
Murrays join forces they'll be that strong they'll be able
to king it from Berwick to Peebles ! Isn't that right,
Thomas ?

THOMAS : [*Reluctantly*] Well, I suppose it is . . . in a worldly
sense. All the same I'm still for the hanging. It's right
traditionally, it's right naturally, and what's most
important—it's right poetically !

MEG : [*Reproachfully*] Thomas !

GRIZEL : Aye, if you think I'm going to have the roof
burnt over my head to make a theme for a gadabout
minstrel's song you're sad mistaken. [*To Gideon*] Well,
Gideon, are you for him [*Pointing to Thomas*] or for me
and Meg ? For a hanging or for a wedding ?

SIR G. : [*Perplexed*] Ach ! I'll not have it ! Maybe you've
got no pride, Grizel Murray, but I'll not throw my
daughter at a Scott's head.

MEG : But I want to be thrown, Father !

SIR G. : Lassie, have you no modesty ?

MEG : This is no time for modesty. It's my last chance.
It's Willie or the embroidery and I hate stitching.

GRIZEL : I'll tell you another thing to recommend it,
Gideon. It'll save a tocher.

SIR G. : Save the dowry ? [*Sees it*] Aye, aye ! There is
something in that. Ach, but it's still blethers. Even if

I did agree to it—and mind you, I'm not saying I do !—
he'd never have her.

GRIZEL : Not even if the alternative was a hanging ?

SIR G. : Aye. That does make a difference. I wonder
now. . . .

GRIZEL : [*Coaxing him*] What about going down to the
dungeon and putting the question to him now ? After
all, there's no use wasting time. I wouldn't put it past
the Scotts to come back the night.

MEG : I wish you would, Father !

SIR G. : Oh, well then. Have it your own ways. [*At the
door*] But mind ! My instincts are all against it. Don't
blame me if things go wrong ! [*He exits*]

THOMAS : [*Disgusted*] Women !

MEG : [*To Grizel*] Do you think he'll have me, Mother ?

GRIZEL : Well, you know what the apostle Paul says,
Meg—Better marry than burn. I suppose it applies to
hanging.

MEG : Oh Mother ! [*She clings to Grizel*]

GRIZEL : [*Softening*] Now, now, my hinny. Don't you take
on now. I'm sorry it's come this way and that you're
missing all the sweet daftness of a courting. But he's a
well-set up lad, Willie, and he looks a good lad, even
if he is wild. You'll see, you'll like him fine and
maybe in time you'll end fonder of him than if you had
begun by daffin.

MEG : [*Withdrawing a little*] Oh, Mother, it's not that.
You don't understand. I'm not just wanting to be
married. I like him. I like him—fine !

THOMAS : Well, it's not my idea of romance !

    [*Enter Gideon*]

SIR G. : Well, I've told him.

GRIZEL : What did he say ?

MEG : Did he say he'd take me ?

SIR G. : He said that he'd think it over, but that as far as his feelings went the night, he was all in favour of the hanging !

SCENE TWO

The Elibank dungeon later the same night. The dungeon is a gloomy cellar with damp glistening stone walls, and its only furnishings are a rough wooden bench and in a corner, a heap of mouldy straw. The door is low and studded with iron nails and has a barred Judas hole. High up on one wall is a tiny barred window through which a shaft of moonlight strikes down on Willie as he sits on the bench, chin on hands, pondering his predicament till the sound of steps in the passage makes him raise his head and look towards the door. A light gleams through the Judas.

WATTIE : [*Off*] Keep your sword handy and let him have it if he tries any games on.

JOCK : [*Off*] Leave him to me, Wattie.

> [*A key grates in the lock and the door creaks open, and Jock enters, in his right hand a sword, in his left a candle. He is followed immediately by Wattie, whose back is bowed under a huge truss of clean straw which he throws on the heap in the corner*]

WATTIE : The mistress said you were to have clean straw. God kens why! The old straw was good enough for Jo Wilson and Hughie when they were here.

WILLIE : A prisoner's entitled to clean straw.

WATTIE : [*Dusting his hands*] Aye, maybe, but what a man's entitled to and what he gets are rarely the same, Willie. Is there anything else you want?

WILLIE: Aye ! Meat.

[*Wattie laughs*]

WATTIE: You'll be for marrying her ?

WILLIE: I'll be hanged if I will !

WATTIE: You'll be hanged if you won't. Take my advice, Willie. Swallow your pride and take her. She's a cosy armful even if her mouth's on the big side and you could march far and fare worse.

WILLIE: I'll not be tricked into wedlock.

WATTIE: Then you'll die a bachelor. Still, it's your funeral. But think it over, Willie. Marriage may be an incurable disease, but hanging's mortal. Come on, Jock, let's out of this. [*To Willie*] Do you want the light ?

WILLIE: Aye, you might as well leave it.

WATTIE: [*Taking candle from Jock and setting it on floor beside the bench*] There you are then. And mind what I said, Willie. Think it over lad. Think it over.

> [*Wattie exits yawning followed by Jock who backs out watchfully. The door grates to, their footsteps echo away and Willie relaxing heaves a deep sigh while his fingers stray to his throat as if he already felt the noose about it. Suddenly he jumps up and takes a step towards the door, then draws himself up abruptly*]

WILLIE: [*Muttering to himself*] No, I'm damned if I'll give in to them.

> [*He returns to the bench and sits down again and a second later there is a faint step outside*]

MEG: [*Speaking through Judas*] Willie !

WILLIE: [*Jumping up*] Who's that ?

MEG: [*Off*] It's me, Willie.

WILLIE: [*Going towards door*] Who's me? What do you want?

MEG: I've got something for you, Willie, but before I open the door will you promise you'll not try to escape?

WILLIE: All right. I promise.

   [*Meg unlocks the door, slips in and locks it behind her again, then hands Willie a cup*]

MEG: That's for you, lad.

WILLIE: What is it?

MEG: A cup of ale. I thought you might be thirsty after the knock you got.

WILLIE: My throat's ablaze. [*Drinks*] Eh, that was good, lass, thank you, lass.

MEG: I'm sorry it's such a wee cup but it was the only one I could find down here. [*Holds up key*] It's lucky I could come at all, but as it happens all the locks down here are the same. This is the key of the winter wood store. But wait, I've something else for you.

   [*She searches in the pocket of her apron and hands him a scone*]

WILLIE: A bannock scone! Lassie, I could kiss you!

MEG: [*Eagerly*] Oh, Willie, I wish you would!

WILLIE: [*Drawing back quick*] What's that you said?

MEG: [*With sigh*] Never mind. It slipped out when I wasn't thinking.

WILLIE: You folk here at Elibank are queer cattle. Still, this isn't a bad bannock—to be cooked in a Murray house. Did you make it?

MEG: Aye, they say I'm a fair hand at the bannock-making.

WILLIE: [*Talking with mouth full*] You are that. You'll

59

be one of the servant lasses, I suppose? Come and sit down.

[*They sit down together on the bench, Meg farthest from the candle*]

MEG: [*As they seat themselves*] Did you not see me in the hall before they brought you down, Willie?

WILLIE: I mind seeing one or two lasses up there but my head was in such a whirl that I couldn't tell one face from another. Still, it doesn't matter. What's your name?

MEG: [*Hesitantly*] I—I'd rather not tell you, Willie. It might make trouble.

WILLIE: Oh! It's all one to me. I'm not that curious. You've got a bonny tongue in your head though. Did anyone ever tell you that?

MEG: No, Willie. Do you really mean it?

WILLIE: I've said it, haven't I? That's one thing I've aye liked in a lass—a sweet voice. [*He bends and picks up the candle, puts his free arm round Meg and tries to turn her to the light, but she turns her face away*] Let's have a look at you.

MEG: [*Trying to hide her face*] No, Willie! Please! Don't bring the light too near. I'm not bonny.

WILLIE: [*Forcing her*] Don't be daft. Come on. Look at me!

MEG: Don't, Willie! You're hurting me! [*He forces her round*] There! You've had your will and now you'll send me away.

WILLIE: [*Taking his arm from around her*]. It's true, you're no beauty.

MEG: I'm sorry, Willie.

WILLIE : Oh, it's not your fault. We can't all be good-looking.

MEG : Some folk think I've got bonny eyes, Willie.

WILLIE : [*With quick glance at them*] Aye, maybe. I've seen worse. [*Looks again*] They're kind eyes. But you've got a muckle mouth on you, lass. You'll be kin to old Murray's daughter, maybe ?

MEG : In a way, Willie.

WILLIE : She must be a frightsome hag, yon one.

MEG : Oh, I wouldn't say that, Willie. She's got bonny eyes too—like mine.

WILLIE : I've heard that she squints something horrible.

MEG : It's a lie ! She doesn't squint. And Willie . . .

WILLIE : Well ?

MEG : She liked you, Willie. She saw you when they brought you up from the pound, all dusty and bloody from the battle, and she liked you fine. She thought you were a braw braw gallant.

WILLIE : Oh well, that's natural enough. The Scotts are all well-fashioned men. She'd have to be pretty cross-eyed not to see that ! But it's not what she thinks that matters : It's what I think.

MEG : You've a good conceit of yourself, haven't you ?

WILLIE : And what for no ? With my lineage ?

MEG : It wasn't for your birth that Meg liked you. She liked you because you were young and braw and not a jot put out by the threat of the hanging.

WILLIE : Huh. It's little she kens. Just thinking of that rope's giving me a sore throat this minute. [*Touches his throat*]. But I wasn't giving anything away before an Elibank Murray.

61

MEG : And you didn't, Willie. You can be sure of that, lad. Oh, you were fine ! Fine ! I couldn't help—I mean Meg couldn't help falling in love with you. She said she couldn't bear the thought of you being hung. I heard her myself.

WILLIE : [*Rising*] I don't find much pleasure in the prospect either so keep off the subject, will you. It's too personal.

MEG : I'll not speak of it if you don't want me to, but I can't help thinking about it. It's an awful death hanging.

WILLIE : It would be an awful life married to Meg.

MEG : You might grow to like her.

WILLIE : I might grow to like hanging.

MEG : [*Loosing grip*] Oh Willie ! Willie ! I wish you'd marry her !

WILLIE : [*Holding her off*] Here ! What's this ? You seem uncommonly interested in this affair ! Meg Murray didn't send you down to speak for her, did she ?

MEG : Oh no, Willie. She wouldn't do a thing like that.

WILLIE : Well, just you look after your own marrying and don't trouble your head about mine. What's it to you what happens to Willie Scott ?

MEG : More than you think. You see, Willie—I hope you'll not think I'm too forward—but I like you myself, lad, and the thought of you dancing in a tow hurts me sore.

WILLIE : Well, don't keep harping on about it ! It hurts me too. I'm too young to die.

MEG : Too young and too braw.

WILLIE : It's not as if I'd done anything ill to merit it either. I mean, what lad worth his salt hasn't done a bit reiving ?

MEG : I ken, Willie. It might happen to anybody.

WILLIE: That's the worst of a family like the Murrays. Not being gentlefolk themselves they don't know how to behave when they run into one.

MEG: [*Her pride pricked*] Oh no! I'll not agree with you there, Willie. The Murrays are as good as the Scotts any day.

WILLIE: Rubbish, lassie! Surely you ken how they got their ground?

MEG: Aye, fine I do. They bought it with honest silver.

WILLIE: Well, doesn't that show you? Now, if they'd been gentlefolk, like the Scotts, they'd have took it.

MEG: I see. I hadn't thought of it like that.

WILLIE: I thought you'd see the difference when I explained it. You're a wise-like lass.

MEG: Do you really think so, Willie?

WILLIE: Oh aye, it's easy to see. Though it beats me how you come by your wit—being a Murray.

MEG: Of course, I'm only half a Murray, Willie.

WILLIE: That explains all!

MEG: Meg's just half a Murray too, Willie.

WILLIE: [*With guffaw*] Which half? The one with the muckle mou'?

MEG: [*Impatiently*] I wish you'd forget about that for five minutes. If you only knew, her mouth's not much bigger than mine.

WILLIE: So you say, but I've heard another story. Besides, if she's not as bad as they say she is, why can't she come down and let me have a look at her? [*Jumps up suddenly and turns towards door*] Is that someone else coming?

MEG: Oh Willie! They mustn't find me here.

WILLIE: Well, you can't get out now. See! Snug down

in the corner there and I'll cover you with straw. Maybe they'll not notice you.

MEG: [*Meg lies down in the straw*] Get rid of them quick, Willie.

WILLIE: Wheest! [*He heaps straw on her*] Keep quiet now. [*He turns away from the straw as a candle is raised to the Judas*]

THOMAS: [*At Judas*] Are you there, Willie?

WILLIE: Where the de'il else would I be?

THOMAS: It's Thomas the Rhymer, Willie. I'm coming in but——

WILLIE: [*Interrupting*] But before you do you want me to promise I'll not try to escape. All right, I promise. Hurry up and get it over.

THOMAS: [*Opening door and then turning to lock it*] You took the words out of my mouth. Just a minute till I lock the door in case anybody tries it in the by-going. There!

WILLIE: Here! I thought you were dead.

THOMAS: Not me! I was just in Elfland.

WILLIE: Oh, was that it? How did you get the key for here?

THOMAS: I happened to ken that all the locks doon here are the same. This is the key of the ale-cellar.

WILLIE: Aye! You would ken that one! Elfland's not changed *you* much.

THOMAS: That it hasn't! But never mind me. Now we're alone at last how are you doing, lad?

WILLIE: Oh passable, passable.

THOMAS: You're keeping your pecker up I hope?

WILLIE: Oh aye, more or less . . .

THOMAS : I'm glad to hear it ! Man, yon was a grand show you put up in the hall the night. I was proud of you, Willie. Proud of you ! Your father would have been proud of you !

WILLIE : I'm glad everybody's pleased.

THOMAS : Aye, it was a grand performance, Willie. It did my heart good to hear you defying old Murray—not a bit daunted by the threat of the hanging.

WILLIE : Hum. To tell you the truth, Thomas, I was so blazing mad at being taken that I didn't know half what I was saying up there.

THOMAS : That's just your modesty, Willie. I ken better. Aye ! I said, listening to you, there's the true border breed coming out at last. There's one lad that there's none'll put down. There's a gallant, I said, that'll go singing to the scaffold !

WILLIE : That's what you said, was it ?

THOMAS : That's what I said, Willie. There's one I said, there's one at least than can live in the old high heroic fashion—aye ! and die in it.

WILLIE : I'm not too set on the dying part.

THOMAS : Make nothing of it, Willie. You'll see, you'll do it fine, lad. I've got great faith in you, Willie.

WILLIE : It's such an undignified death, hanging.

THOMAS : But you'll make it dignified. [*In joyous anticipation*] Oh, I can see it all : Meg lying on the stones in a dead faint ; Grizel pleading with you to give way ; Murray frowning, black as thunder, and you up there, laughing in his face, the gibbet under you like a golden throne and the noose about your neck like a golden collar ! Oh, Willie, it'll be just grand !

65   E

WILLIE : That's all very well but what if it's me that's doing the pleading and Murray the laughing ?

THOMAS : [*Confidentially*] Well [*Looking around*] strictly between us two, Willie, I'll promise you now that if your natural feelings should overcome you for a minute, I'll not say a word of it in the verses.

WILLIE : Verses ? What verses ?

THOMAS : My ballad, man. I'm making up a ballad about you. If you'll *just* do your bit it'll be my masterpiece. Such pathos in the lines that describe your end, Willie. There's nothing like it in the minstrelsy of the borders. It would bring tears to the eyes of an Edinburgh lawyer.

WILLIE : You're making up a ballad about *me* ?

THOMAS : Am I not telling you ! If you'll just let yourself be hanged, Willie, I'll make you immortal !

WILLIE : I'm not sure I want to be immortal for a while yet. You're in too much of a hurry, Thomas.

THOMAS : Here, you're not weakening, are you ? Man I'll never forgive you if you let me down now.

WILLIE : Let you down ! What about me ? What's a ballad to me if I can't hear it ?

THOMAS : That's no way at all to look at it, Willie Scott. You should be proud of the chance to provide the raw material for such a masterpiece.

WILLIE : Well, maybe you're right, but I can't see it that way. Can you not give your ballad a different ending ?

THOMAS : No, no. It can't be done. I've thought it all out and there's just the one end possible. The whole conception of the poem hangs on the one peg—your noble refusal to save your neck at the cost of liberty. [*There is a rustle in the straw*] Is that a rat there ?

66

WILLIE: I suppose it is.

THOMAS: Well, can I count on you?

WILLIE: Count on me for what?

THOMAS: To hang out to the bitter end, man! To defy the Murrays to the courts of heaven or the gates of hell?

WILLIE: Oh, no. I'm not making any promises, Thomas. What you don't seem to understand is that this is a serious matter for me. I must think about it.

THOMAS: Losh! Willie, but that's the one thing you mustn't do! If you start thinking you're lost, man. Lost! You might as well go up crawling to Gideon now and throw your hand in.

WILLIE: Don't be daft, Thomas. A lad's got to think whiles.

THOMAS: Rubbish! I give not a cast clout for your thinking. Do you suppose any of the great tragic situations of the world would ever have come about if folk had sat down and taken time for consideration? Never a one of them! Think of the old Greeks and yon lassie Helen! Do you imagine they'd have hung about all these years on the plains of Troy if they'd given a moment's thought to the matter? Not them! If they'd started thinking they'd have up-sails and away, never caring a docken whether she bedded with Paris or Menelaus! Why, man, I often wonder if the good Lord Himself wouldn't have stopped the work of creation on the night of the fifth day if He'd given full consideration to the awful consequences that would follow the rest of it! No, no, Willie, don't you start thinking or you'll be married to Meg before you can cry " Barley."

WILLIE: What's she really like—Meg? Is she as ill-favoured as they say she is?

THOMAS: Now that's a difficult question to answer. I wouldn't like to say anything against the lassie behind her back.

WILLIE: Then, is she *not* as ill-favoured as they say she is? Can you answer that?

THOMAS: [*In difficulties*] Well, she's . . . [*To himself*] Oh! Damn the Queen of Elfland!

WILLIE: What's that you said?

THOMAS: Nothing, nothing. I was thinking about another lassie.

WILLIE: Put your other lasses out of your head and stick to the subject of Meg. And answer me straight this time. Is she better or worse than they say she is?

THOMAS: [*Hesitantly*] She's got all her members, Willie. In justice I'll say that.

WILLIE: [*Impatiently*] So have a cross-eyed cow and a splay-footed mare!

THOMAS: [*Quickly*] Exactly! That's just what I meant. [*Straw rustles*] My! There must be a herd of rats in that straw.

WILLIE: Never mind the rats! Keep your mind on Meg Murray and tell me this now. Does she squint?

THOMAS: Och, Willie, it's not for me to say that any lassie squints. [*Making for door*] I think I'll be getting away.

WILLIE: [*Getting between Thomas and door*] Oh no, you don't. You're not leaving here till you answer me. And I don't want to hear about any other lassie. I want to hear about Meg Murray. *Does she squint?*

THOMAS : Oh, damn it all then, she does——

> [*There is a chord of harp music and the Elfin Queen, finger raised warningly at Thomas, materialises in a green light through the dungeon wall*]

THE L.I.G. : Thomas !

THOMAS : [*Cringing*] She doesn't squint !

> [*The Elfin Queen fades out smiling. Willie, who has seen and heard nothing, looks from Thomas to the wall and back at Thomas, completely mystified*]

WILLIE : What's the matter with you ? You're awful jumpy. Oh, but this is very interesting. Maybe Meg's not splay-footed either ?

THOMAS : Well, as a matter of fact [*He glances apprehensively at the place where the Lady in Green appeared and sees a faint greeny glow beginning to show*] she's not !

> [*The green glow fades out*]

WILLIE : Uh-huh ! I'm beginning to think Meg Murray's not the flipperty-gibbet she's made out to be.

THOMAS : Willie Scott, I warned you ! You're thinking, and if you think you're lost !

WILLIE : I tell you I've got to think !

THOMAS : Then think of her muckle mouth, Willie. Think of the laughing in the Selkirk taverns if you take *her* to wife.

WILLIE : I'd soon sort anybody that laughed at me !

THOMAS : Aye, if you caught them at it. But most times you wouldn't. But you'd be aware of it all the same and you wouldn't like it, Willie. No lad likes to be laughed at. You wouldn't lay yourself open to that, Willie ?

WILLIE : I've not said I would, have I ? All the same it's

very interesting to hear that Meg's not the hag she's
cracked up to be. Maybe even her mouth's not so
monstrous? Come on, be honest?

THOMAS: [*Reluctantly*] Well, you couldn't stall a cow in it,
that's true enough. Not a common-sized cow anyway.
[*Rustle in straw*] My! These rats'll be over nipping our
shins in a minute.

WILLIE: 1 wouldn't wonder. [*He turns to the door*] Sounds
like more visitors.

> [*Sir Gideon is heard groaning and coughing in the corridor*]

THOMAS: [*In great alarm*] Good God! It's Sir Gideon.
Where can 1 hide, Willie? If the Laird finds me here
I'll get my head in my hands. [*He tries to creep under
the bench*]

WILLIE: [*Hauling him out*] Come out there you daft skite!
Come on! You'll have to get into the straw too—if
you're not afraid of the rats!

THOMAS: De'il take the rats! It's Sir Gideon I'm
afraid of. [*Thomas plunges into the corner and Willie
kicks straw over him. Sir Gideon raises his candle to the
Judas*].

SIR G.: Are you there, Willie?

WILLIE: Aye, I'm here and if you're wanting my promise
not to escape when you open the door, you can take it
for granted.

> [*Willie goes over and sits down on the bench. Sir G.
> comes in. He is wearing a white nightshirt over which
> he has belted his sword, and has a red stocking cap on
> his head*]

SIR G.: How did you ken I was going to say that?

WILLIE: My grandfather was a warlock.

SIR G.: I never heard tell of it. Still, it doesn't matter. That wasn't what I came to talk about.

WILLIE: Well, whatever it was I hope that you'll say it quick. You folk at Elibank don't seem to be very fond of your beds.

SIR G.: Everybody's sleeping sound now, Willie, everybody except ourselves and the watchman. I'm sorry to come down so late but I wanted a word with you in strict privacy. [*Edging on to bench*] Do you mind if I sit down? Old age is creeping on you know, creeping on.

WILLIE: Oh, make yourself at home. Don't mind me.

SIR G.: [*Clearing his throat*] Thank you, Willie. Eh, those damp airs don't do my chest any good [*Coughs*]. I hope you're quite comfortable yourself, lad?

WILLIE: That depends on what you mean by comfortable.

SIR G.: I see they've given you clean straw. That's good. I wouldn't like you to catch a chill here.

WILLIE: [*Turning to him*] Just what are you after, Murray?

SIR G.: Me? Oh, I'm not after anything! I simply looked down to make sure all was well with you. Eh, but this bench could be softer. I'll have a cushion sent down to you first thing in the morning, Willie—if you're still here that is.

WILLIE: [*Suspiciously*] What does that mean exactly?

SIR G.: Well you ken Grizel and I'll be right glad to welcome you up in the hall as soon as you've made up your mind to the wedding.

WILLIE: Ha! You'll wait a long time before that happens!

SIR G.: You're still against it then?

WILLIE: I'm dead set against it.

SIR G.: [*Looking at straw*] Is that a rat in the straw, Willie?

WILLIE : You should know. It's your straw.

SIR G. : I thought we had cleared them all out. But what was I saying ? Oh aye, about the wedding. I'm sorry you feel that way about it. Don't be too hasty in making up your mind, lad. You're in an awkward predicament —in fact we're all in an awkward predicament and well, to cut a long tale short, I've a proposition to put to you, Willie.

WILLIE : Oh ?

SIR G. : About the tocher, lad. The tocher.

WILLIE : I thought you said there was to be no tocher ?

SIR G. : [*Coughing*] Aye, I believe I did, I believe I did. But I don't want to be too hard on you, and well, I've been thinking it over and though there'll be no tocher, officially—I can't go back on my word you see—I'm prepared—if you decide on the wedding—and mind I'm not pressing you !—it makes no odds to me if you'd rather be hanged—I'm prepared, as I said, to hand over [*Largely*] Whinnock Braes to you as a wedding gift ! [*Looking at straw*] Losh ! I can hardly hear myself speaking for these rats. Wait a bit till I settle them.

> [*Sir Gideon draws his sword and is going to slash at the heap of straw when Willie grabs at his arm*]

WILLIE : Hold on, for God's sake !

SIR G. : What's the matter with you ? You don't want a rout of rats playing ring-o-roses on your chest, do you ?

WILLIE : Leave the beasts alone. I'm fond of them.

SIR G. : Fond of rats ? Rats ? Well, well, I suppose we all have our pleasures ! [*Sheaths sword*] And now what do you say to my proposition ?—to Whinnock Braes ?

WILLIE : You're generous, aren't you ? Whinnock Braes

is a stoneyard. All you could raise on it would be a
crop of thorn!

SIR G. : Well, you can burn thorn, can't you? Kindling's
always useful in a house. However, since you're not
satisfied I'll throw in the Water Meadow along with it.

WILLIE : [*Showing interest*] The east one?

SIR G. : No! The best cattle ground south of Lauder?
Do you think I'm soft? The *west* one.

WILLIE : Away with you, Murray! The West Meadow's a
marsh!

SIR G. : Not in the dry season, Willie. There's a good bite
for many a beast there in the dry season.

WILLIE : Aye, for the web-footed kind!

SIR G. : All right! all right! I've no wish to influence
you one way or the other. [*Rises*] But mind, Willie, if
you bide stubborn you'll hang. You'll hang if it's the
last thing I do.

WILLIE : If I ken my brothers that's just what it will
be.

SIR G. : Maybe so, Willie, maybe so, but that'll not help
you when you're keeping house with the moles! [*Looks
to door*] Was that a step?

WILLIE : It was, and you can't hide in the straw, Murray.
There's no room.

SIR G. : What the de'il would I hide in the straw for?

WILLIE : Oh, I just thought you might want to.

SIR G. : You're cracked, man.

WILLIE : Then I'm in the right place for there's a deal of
daft folk in this house from what I've seen the night.

[*Enter Grizel in her nightgown and with her hair in
paper curlers*]

73

GRIZEL: [*To Gideon*] Are you coming to your bed or are you here for the night?

SIR G.: I'm just coming, Grizel. [*Coughs*]

GRIZEL: It's about time. This is no place for a man with a cold.

SIR G.: Aye, you're right there. I'm just wasting my time anyway. I've been trying to make this laddie see reason but I can't shift him. Can I give you my arm up the stair, Grizel? [*Offers it*].

GRIZEL: [*Drawing back*] Have you been drinking again. Gideon? Away up the stair yourself and don't make an exhibition of yourself. I'll have a word with Willie myself while I'm here.

SIR G.: It's a waste of breath, Grizel.

GRIZEL: We'll see, we'll see.

SIR G.: Well, don't be too long. You always wake me up when you come in after me.

> [*Sir Gideon exits yawning. Grizel sits on the bench with Willie*]

GRIZEL: Now, Willie, let's have a wee confab. You're not weary, are you?

WILLIE: Well, no, but I would like to sleep sometime. Was there anything particular you wanted?

GRIZEL: No no, nothing particular, Willie. I just thought it would be a comfort to you to know you had one friend in the house.

WILLIE: Have I?

GRIZEL: Aye, Willie. Whatever happens you can trust to me to do my best for you. By the by did Gideon make you any sort of a proposition when he was here?

WILLIE: I wasn't interested.

GRIZEL: Oh, then he did make you a proposal. What was it Willie? The East Water Meadow?

WILLIE: No! The west one!

GRIZEL: The west one? It's not worth a sheaf of bindweed. But isn't that just like Gideon: giving away what's of no use to him with a grand flourish! And was that all he offered you?

WILLIE: He tried to palm off Whinnock Braes on me.

GRIZEL: What! That rabbit warren? You did right well to turn them down flat, Willie. But never mind these small matters. Tell me, how are you feeling about the wedding generally, lad?

WILLIE: I'm not feeling anything about it, Lady Grizel. As far as I'm concerned there's not going to be a wedding.

GRIZEL: You're not wishful to be hanged, Willie?

WILLIE: No, but I'm not wishful to be married either— leastways to Meg Murray.

GRIZEL: Oh and what, may I ask, might be wrong with Meg Murray?

WILLIE: Ach, you know very well what's wrong with her, Lady Grizel.

[*Grizel rises*]

GRIZEL: Willie Scott! You don't mean to tell me that a lad of your intelligence has been taken in by these lies about Meg's looks? Ah! I see I've been mistaken in you and that being so I might as well get up to my bed. [*Turns to go to door*]

WILLIE: Just a minute! Are the tales not true then?

GRIZEL: False as the tongues that spread them! Yon's nothing but tavern talk and backstairs blethers, Willie.

There's not a sweeter lass than our Meg in Scotland. As for her mouth . . . well, I'll not say it's a wee mouth but what's so bonny about a wee mouth? It's the sign of a mean ungenerous disposition. Look at Gideon!

WILLIE: Huh! You've made a point there! But see here. There's no smoke without flame. If Meg's not so ill-favoured as they make out why can't I have a look at her?

GRIZEL: Willie Scott, what do you think the lassie is? A heifer at auction to be poked in the ribs and looked up and down before you make a bid for her? Oh no! I wouldn't let Meg demean herself that way. If you want to marry her you'll first have to make up your mind to it. Then you'll have to ask her. Aye, and then she'll have to accept you.

WILLIE: Accept me? Does she not want me then?

GRIZEL: She hasn't made up her mind yet. It would be a real pity if she wouldn't have you, Willie. Gideon would have no option but to hang you then.

WILLIE: [Confused] Lady Grizel, you've got it all wrong!

GRIZEL: How Willie?

WILLIE: It's not Meg that's to choose between a wedding and a hanging—it's me!

GRIZEL: I fear that it's you that's got it wrong, Willie. It would be Gideon that misled you. He's got no gift for explaining, Gideon. It's true that you've got to marry Meg or be hanged, but you can't marry Meg if she's not willing so it's her choice too. Still I'm hopeful, Willie. I'll not say Meg's in love with you but she's heart-sorry for you and that's well on the way to it. And as I said before you can trust me at least to do my

best for both of you. As for the tocher, pay no heed
to Gideon. If Meg does decide to have you I'll see to
it she doesn't come to you empty-handed. The West
Meadow indeed! She'll have the East Meadow, Willie.
Aye, and the Greenacre ground beyond the hill along
with it. Now I'm off to my bed. Good night, lad, and
don't be down-hearted. I'll do all I can for you with
Meg.

> [*Willie is so flabbergasted by these words that he can only
> gape as he listens to them. At the close Lady Grizel
> exits with much dignity. And as she goes Willie follows
> her, making protesting gestures, to the door*]

WILLIE : But Lady Grizel——

> [*But the door closes and Lady Grizel has gone. There is
> a rustle in the straw as Thomas sits up*]

THOMAS : Are they all gone ?

WILLIE : Aye, and it's time you were off too. I'm fed up
with visitors !

THOMAS : [*Rising and to Willie whom he takes by the arm*]
Willie Scott, what's in that straw ?

WILLIE : Is it not rats, then ?

THOMAS : If it is, they've got leather shoes on and they've
been kick-kicking at me for the last half hour. [*Goes
back to straw, grabs Meg's arms and drags her out*] Why !
it's a lassie.

MEG : Thomas ! You're hurting me. Let me go !

WILLIE : Leave her be, Thomas.

THOMAS : [*Dragging Meg to candle*] I'll not hurt her—I just
want to have a look at her. By old Blind Harry ! It's
Meg Murray !

WILLIE : What !

ACT III

Early morning : between two towers on the battlements of the castle, two days later. Over the battlements rises the topmost boughs of a tall tree and beyond are rounded green hills and a clear blue sky. Wattie is hammering into position a support for the main post of a gibbet which has been erected on a raised platform, in a central bay of the battlements, and the rope, the noose of which hangs over the wall, is already in position. Seated on a bench, at one side, Thomas is writing with a quill on a crackling parchment, and as Wattie gives a particularly heavy blow with his hammer, he looks up, frowning.

THOMAS : Are you not nearly done there ? How do you expect me to work in such a din ?

WATTIE : [*Looking round post*] I've got to fix it, haven't I ? It would be a fine thing if it broke under him.

THOMAS : Broke ? That gibbet would hold an elephant !

WATTIE : And what might an elephant be when it's at home ?

THOMAS : Man, but you're ignorant. Have you never heard of that great beast the elephant ?

WATTIE : Not me.

THOMAS : It's the grandest beast in the world, Wattie— about the size and shape of a two storey house, with a tail at each end of it.

WATTIE : Get away with you !

THOMAS : It's the truth I'm telling you. And that's not all, Wattie. Besides that, it's got two front teeth more

than six feet long and squirts water through its front
tail and the one thing in the world that it's frightened
of is a mouse.

WATTIE : [*Ironically*] It doesn't sing the Borderer's Lament
for the Dead Cow through its back tail by any chance ?

THOMAS : I'm not joking, Wattie. It's a real beast this.

WATTIE : [*Sceptically*] Aye, aye. [*Comes down from platform
with hammer over his shoulder. He leans over Thomas to look
at his MSS*] What's this you're at ?

THOMAS : Just my ballad.

WATTIE : The one about the raid ?

THOMAS : Aye, it's on the last stretch now. If all goes well
I'll carp it over to you in the hall to-night.

WATTIE : [*Pointing*] What does that bit say ?

THOMAS : Can't you read ?

WATTIE : Me ? I leave that sort of thing to the women !

THOMAS : More ignorance ! This is the bit where I tell
how the Murrays went down to the dungeon to plead
with Willie to marry Meg, and how he spurned all their
offers. Will I say it over to you ?

WATTIE : Aye, you might as well. Say that bit there with
the wee hills in it.

THOMAS : That's not hills, you gomeril ! It's a W for
Willie. But hark now and tell me how this sounds
to you.

[*Rising and reading with great expression*]

" Then loudly answered the gallant Willie
  ' Freely I lived and free will dee
   Though I may hang from your gallows Murray
   Your daughter's gudeman I'll never be.

" Mirk, mirk is this dungeon here
   But you will never daunten me,
   No Scott has yet bow'd down to a Murray
   And I shall ne'er bow down to thee.' "

How's that ?

WATTIE : [*Not impressed*] Umm. It's passable. What comes after that ?

THOMAS : That's all I've done so far. The next part describes the hanging. [*Looking around*] It's a pity it's such a grand morning. It would have been more in keeping if there had been a thunderstorm on the way. And yet, maybe not, maybe not. It aye makes a contrast. A blue sky and the birds singing and in the midst of it the poor lad choking in his death agony. Aye, I should be able to make something of that ! Let's see. How would this do ?

    [*While Thomas is reciting and Wattie listening to him,
    Meg enters with a coil of rope in her hand, flits unobserved
    across the scene and disappears behind one of the towers*]

" The throstles sang in every bush
   The merles in every tree
   There was no cloud in the blue blue sky
   No stain on the blue blue sea.

" There was no cloud in the blue blue sky
   No stain on the blue blue sea
   When they opened the door of the dungeon grim
   And led Willie out to dee."

THOMAS : How does that strike you, Wattie ?

WATTIE : I'm not much taken with all these " blue blues."
And I'm hanged if I can hear any birds singing.

THOMAS : They're singing in my head, man. Flocks of
them !

WATTIE : Oh, is that the way of it ! I've often wondered
how you rhymer lads could aye hear a hoolit or a clap
of thunder when you wanted one. So that's the way
of it, is it ?

THOMAS : That's the way of it, Wattie. It's what's called
the poetic licence. [*The Harp of Elfland sounds*] Oh, losh !
I'm away again !

WATTIE : What's wrong with you now ?

THOMAS : I've lost my licence ! [*Crossing to battlements*]
There's surely one bird in sight ? Just one and I'd
risk it.

WATTIE : I can't see a tail feather.

> [*Thomas whistles to attract birds and after a moment
> a cuckoo answers him*]

WATTIE : [*Delighted*] There's one !

THOMAS : [*Making a face*] It'll not do. [*Goes back to his
bench in a very ill temper*].

> [*Enter Sir Gideon from the left*]

WATTIE : Morning, Sir Gideon. It's a grand day for the
hanging.

SIR G. : I'm not looking forward to it with the pleasure
I'd expected. [*Looking at gibbet*] Is that thing ready ?

WATTIE : Aye, there she is—as good a job as I've ever
done.

SIR G. : Is it all right in the corner there ? It doesn't look
firm-set to me.

WATTIE : It's sure founded as the Bass Rock, Laird. As Thomas says you could hang a—what was the name of yon beast, Thomas ?

THOMAS : An elephant.

WATTIE : That's it. You could hang an elephant on it.

SIR G. : What for ?

WATTIE : What for what ?

SIR G. : What for would you hang an elephant on it ?

WATTIE : What do you hang anything on one of these things for ? To get quit of it, naturally !

SIR G. : [*Looking for it*] Where is this elephant ?

THOMAS : It's a metaphorical elephant, Laird.

SIR G. : [*Angrily*] I don't care if it's a Scandinavian elephant ! It's no right here. Is it yours, Thomas ?

THOMAS : There's no elephant, Sir Gideon. It's a figure of speech. All Wattie means is that the gibbet's strong enough to hang an elephant on if you wanted to hang an elephant on it.

[*Sir G. looks from Thomas to Wattie, still suspicious*]

WATTIE : That's right, Laird.

SIR G. : [*Giving it up*] Bah ! You're blethering. Bringing up elephants at a time like this ! Oh ! [*He clutches the hollow of his back*]

THOMAS : What's wrong ?

SIR G. : It's my back, Thomas. It's been fair giving me gyp this morning. I was just daft to go out fighting the other night. Fighting's all right when you've got your health and strength but when you come to my age it does you no good, I don't care what anybody says.

WATTIE : Ach, you enjoyed yourself fine.

SIR G. : While it lasted, Wattie, while it lasted ! But

what's half an hour's pleasure when you set it against the hours of agony I've been having since ? Here ! Let me sit down.

> [*Thomas rises and Sir Gideon takes his place*].

THOMAS : All the same, Sir Gideon, you've got one consolation. If you hadn't gone out the other night you wouldn't have caught Willie Scott and I'd have no ballad. So you can congratulate yourself that, in a left-handed sort of way, you've made a contribution to the glories of Scottish minstrelsy.

SIR G. : [*Gloomily*] I wish to heaven I'd never set eyes on Willie Scott.

THOMAS : That's a queer thing to say ! What makes you wish that ?

SIR G. : Don't be so mealy-mouthed, Thomas. You know fine why ! [*Mops his brow*] They're laughing at me from here to Peebles. Gideon Murray—the man with the daughter that's worse than a hanging ! Ech, I'll never dare to set my foot beyond my own boundary line after this. It'll be the death of me this morning's work. You'll see it will.

WATTIE : I'll tell you one thing, Laird. The Scotts'll not be laughing.

SIR G. : No, they'll be out for blood. Oh, but it's an awful predicament. If it wasn't that folk might think I was scared of the Scotts I'd call the whole thing off.

THOMAS : You'd better not !

SIR G. : [*Jumping up*] Who the devil are you to say what I'll do or not do ?

THOMAS : [*Solemnly*] Sir Gideon, I've nothing against you and I've nothing against Willie Scott. But I need a hanging to finish my ballad and I'm not going to be cheated out of it now! If you go back on your word I swear I'll make up such a rhyme about you that the laughter o' folk when they hear it will shake Elibank stone from stone and leave you standing naked in the winds of derision!

SIR G. : And what if I hang *you*, Thomas? Have you thought of that?

THOMAS : You wouldn't dare! There's never been a rhymer hung yet.

SIR G. : Well, take care you don't make a precedent!

THOMAS : [*Turning contemptuously away*] Huh! [*Turns away*]

WATTIE : [*Pacifically*] Of course there's just the chance Willie might change his mind even yet.

SIR G. : Not him, Wattie. He's the most stubborn young cockerel I've ever encountered. He'll let himself be hung to spite us. [*Sighs*] This is what comes of paying heed to women!

    [*Enter Grizel*]

GRIZEL : And what, may I ask, have the women been doing now?

SIR G. : I was saying I would never have been in this quandary if it hadn't been for that daft notion of yours and Meg's.

GRIZEL : There was nothing daft about the notion, Gideon. If you hadn't been so tight-fisted in the business of the tocher, it would have worked out fine.

SIR G. : Woman! You said yourself it would save the tocher!

GRIZEL : Aye, but that was just to get you moving. I knew that was the one argument would touch you.

SIR G. : Bah! You'd drive a man daft. Here! Let's get it over with. Away down and fetch the prisoner.

WATTIE : Right you are, Laird. [*Exits*]

GRIZEL : Have you seen Meg, Gideon?

SIR G. : Not me. Have you seen her, Thomas?

THOMAS : She's not been up here.

GRIZEL : She's not downstairs either. I wonder where she's hidden herself?

SIR G. : She'll be lying in bed with the sheets over her head—chicken-hearted like all women when it comes to the hard facts of life.

GRIZEL : Well, it's not a bonny sight to see a man hanged. I never cared for it greatly myself.

SIR G. : Life wasn't made for pleasure, Grizel. Still, there's no need for you to stay if it turns your stomach.

GRIZEL : Oh, I'll see it out. It's right and proper I should be here and it'll always help me from feeling ill-done by when the Scotts come seeking their own again.

SIR G. : Do you think they will, Grizel?

GRIZEL : Do you doubt it? The Scotts have never let a feud drop yet and there's an awful lot of them. You're going to have a brisk life of it the next two or three years, Gideon—if you live that long!

SIR G. : You're cheery, aren't you?

GRIZEL : Well, a woman's got to face up to the hard facts of life even if she is a wee thing chicken-hearted whiles.

[*Enter Wattie leading Willie Scott by a rope round his neck and with Jock armed with a pike bringing up the rear. Willie's arms are tied behind his back but despite this he manages to walk with a swagger and is almost offensively cheerful*]

85

WILLIE: Morning, Lady Grizel! Morning, Murray! Morning, Thomas!

THOMAS: Good morning, Willie.

SIR G.: You're very cheerful in the circumstances.

WILLIE: What circumstances?

SIR G.: [*Indicating gibbet*] These circumstances.

WILLIE: [*Glancing at it*] Oh that! You can take it down, Murray. I don't think you'll need it.

SIR G.: Oh?

GRIZEL: You're going to marry her, Willie?

WILLIE: Aye, I've decided to take the plunge, Lady Grizel. [*With bow*] If Meg's willing, that is?

THOMAS: Damnation! There goes my ballad! [*To Willie*] I thought you were a man!

SIR G.: [*Pulling Thomas back*] You keep out of this, Thomas! Wattie, take the ropes off Maister Scott at once.

WILLIE: (*Backing towards gibbet*) Not so fast, Murray! You've not heard all I've to say yet.

GRIZEL: Tuts, tuts, laddie. We can hear the rest at breakfast. See, let me take the ropes off you.

WILLIE: [*Straining back against gibbet platform*] Let the ropes be, Lady Grizel. Maybe Sir Gideon won't be wanting them off when he hears what I've got to say to him. [*Grizel draws back*] This is what it mounts up to, Murray. I'm willing, in the circumstances, [*Looks up at noose*] to take your daughter to wife—but on conditions.

SIR G.: Well, out with it, man! What are your conditions?

THOMAS: Don't chaffer with him, Sir Gideon. It's undignified.

SIR G. : I'm not chaffering with him. It's him that's chaffering with me ! Go on. What's your conditions ?

WILLIE : She's got to bring a good tocher with her or I can't go on with it.

SIR G. : Now, Willie Scott, I've said all I've got to say on that subject. I said there would be no tocher and there'll be no tocher. You must just trust me doing my best for you in the way of a free-given wedding gift.

GRIZEL : It's just a matter of words, Willie.

WILLIE : Maybe so, Lady Grizel, but I'm not taking any chances. I want the kind of wedding gift we're to have made clear now—before witnesses.

THOMAS : You needn't look at me, Willie Scott. I've done with you. I was never so disappointed in a man in my life.

WILLIE : A boddle I care ! Lady Grizel's a good enough witness for me. I can trust her.

GRIZEL : [*Pleased*] That's real nice of you to say that, Willie.

SIR G. : Here ! Whose side are you on ?

WILLIE : Well, Murray, what's it to be ?

SIR G. : As I told you before I'll give you Whinnock Braes and the East Water Meadow and—I'm soft in the head to do it—but well, well, I'll throw in a dozen cows along with them ! Will that satisfy you ?

WILLIE : It will not. Och, I see I'm wasting my time here. [*With jerk of his head to gibbet*] Thomas ! Give's a hoist up, will you ?

THOMAS : What ! Are you going on with it ? Man, I take back every word I said ! [*Helps Willie up on gibbet plat-*

form] Now, don't open your mouth again or you'll spoil it !

WILLIE : I've nothing more to say if Murray hasn't.

[*Grizel whispers urgently in Sir Gideon's ear*]

WILLIE : I wish you'd hurry up. There's a cold wind up here.

SIR G. : [*Indignantly*] I will not !

[*Grizel whispers again*]

SIR G. : Well, we'll be burnt out then !

[*Grizel whispers yet again*]

WILLIE : How's the ballad, Thomas ?

THOMAS : Fine, Willie, fine ! Just you hold on and it'll be a wonder.

SIR G. : [*Breaking away from Grizel, and obviously deeply shocked*] Ye wouldn't do that, Grizel ?

GRIZEL : [*With toss of her head*] I mean it, Gideon.

GIDEON : [*After pause*] Oh, well ! Listen, Willie, you can have the East Meadow and the Green Knowe, and I hope that'll satisfy you.

WILLIE : It's a start at any rate. Now, about stock for the ground. I'll want the wee black bull and——

SIR G. : [*Ominous*] *You'll want what ?*

WILLIE : Are you hard of hearing ? I said I'll want the wee black bull. It's getting old but there's a year or two's service in it yet, doubtless. Then I'll need half a dozen good milking cows, about——

SIR G. : Stop ! I've heard just enough of what you're wanting. I know what you're wanting and by God ! I'll give you it. [*To Grizel*] And don't you try to put me off ! I'll not listen to you. Wattie ! Up you get and put the rope on him.

WATTIE: I thought you'd come to it in the hinder-end. [*He climbs up and fits the noose round Willie's neck*] There you are, Willie. Fits you like a glove. [*He jumps down and takes the free end of the rope in his hands*] Will I swing him off, Laird?

SIR G.: Wait for the word. Now, listen, Willie, I'll give you one last chance. I'll count up to ten and if you haven't come to your senses by then, by thunder! You're by with it!

WILLIE: You can save your breath. I'm immovable! [*Looks down and shutting his eyes sways dizzily*].

SIR G.: Are you ready, Wattie?

WATTIE: Aye, aye, Laird.

SIR G.: Right then. I'll start. [*Slowly with long pauses*] One . . . two . . . three . . . four . . . five . . . six . . . You'd better make up your mind, Willie. You're half-way to eternity. [*Willie sniffs scornfully*] Seven . . . Ei——

THOMAS: [*Enthusiastically*] Hold on, Willie. You're doing fine!

SIR G.: [*Exploding*] Will you keep out of this, Thomas! Eight . . . Nine . . .

> [*Wattie puts his foot against the gibbet and prepares to take the strain on the rope. Willie looks tense but still will not give in. Sir Gideon raises his hand*].

SIR G.: [*Unable to bring himself to it*] Nine!

> [*Wattie almost ruptures himself to avoid pulling the rope and throws Sir Gideon an indignant look but Sir Gideon is too unhappy to notice. Slowly, reluctantly he raises his hand for what can only, this time, be the fatal number, but even as he draws breath to say " ten " Meg appears, perched perilously on the very lip of the parapet. She*

too has a rope about her neck, the far end of which is attached to the tower above]

MEG : Stop !

[*Everyone swings round at her cry and Willie heaves a huge sigh of relief*]

SIR G. : Meg ! What are you doing up there ?

GRIZEL : [*In great alarm*] Come down, bairn ! You'll fall !

MEG : Don't come near me, Mother. I won't fall but if you come near me I'll jump. I swear I will !

WATTIE : She's off her head !

MEG : No, I'm not, Wattie. It's my father that's off his head.

GRIZEL : Hear ! Hear !

SIR G. : Well, I'm——

MEG : You should be black-ashamed at yourself, Father ! Would you put the life of a braw lad like Willie before a herd of cattle and a green field ?

SIR G. : It's not me that's making a stir about cattle and ground. It's him !

MEG : Willie's just insisting on his rights. You wouldn't have me going to him empty-handed, would you ?

[*Sir G. jumps with rage*]

SIR G. : He's not getting my wee black bull ! I'll hang him first !

MEG : Are you dead set on the wee black bull, Willie ?

WILLIE : Aye, Meg. I'm not backing down an inch !

MEG : Well, in that case it's up to you, Father. Do we get the wee black bull or do we jump ?

SIR G. : You wouldn't dare !

MEG : I'm a desperate woman, Father. If I can't live with Willie I'll not live without him !

SIR G.: I ken what I'll do. I'll call the whole thing off! Another day or two in the dungeon on bread and water'll change his opinions. Wattie——

MEG: Stay where you are, Wattie! No, Father. You can't get out of it like that. This affair's got to be settled now and quickly: I don't feel too steady up here! [*She sways and Grizel gasps*].

GRIZEL: Meg! Gideon, do you want to kill her? You'll have to give in sooner or later so you might as well do it now.

SIR G.: [*Folding his arms*] I'll never give in.

GRIZEL: You've got to do something. We can't stay up here for the rest of our lives!

MEG: [*Looking into distance*] Aye, and you'd better do something quick, Father. Here's some visitors coming.

SIR G.: [*Hurrying to battlements*] Visitors? Where?

[*There is a general movement to the battlements*]

WATTIE: There they are!—by the three elms. There's five—no! six of them.

WILLIE: [*Joyously*] It's my old man. I knew he'd come. Now you're for it, Murray!

GRIZEL: I told you you wouldn't have to wait long, Gideon.

SIR G.: Is there just six of them? They're cracked, Wattie. We'll make hash of them!

GRIZEL: Wait! Who's that in the middle? Him on the black horse. I'll swear I ken him.

MEG: Oh mother, it's our Andra! They've got Andra with them. I can see the ropes on his hands.

SIR G.: Thunder and lightning! I never thought of that! Who's that riding forward, Wattie?

WATTIE : It looks like——

WILLIE : It's the old man ! You can come down, Meg. It's all right now.

MEG : Aye, I suppose it is.

> [*But Meg does not come down. A thud of hooves is heard and sounds of a horse being drawn up under the wall*]

THE SCOTT : Hallo there, Murray. A word with you !

MURRAY : Well, Scott, what do you want ?

THE SCOTT : [*Below*] I want our Willie and I want him quick ! And you can go down on your knees and thank God he's not harmed.

SIR G. : And what if I hang him before your eyes, Scott ? As he well deserves !

THE SCOTT : Try it and there'll be four dirks in your son Andra before Willie starts swinging. You're beat, Murray ! You're beat and you'd best admit it.

GRIZEL : He's right, Gideon. Now, don't take any risks.

SIR G. : Bah ! [*Over battlements*] All right, Scott. I'll give you best this time. I might have kent you'd think up some dirty trick like this. All right ! I'll change you Willie for Andra.

THE SCOTT : Fair enough ! Send Willie down !

SIR G. : Oh no ! You bring Andra up !

THE SCOTT : Very well. I'll off for him now.

> [*The Scott is heard riding off*]

SIR G. : Here ! I've had enough of this. Come down out of that, Willie.

WILLIE : Aye, I might as well.

> [*Wattie lifts the noose off Willie's head and helps him down then takes off his other ropes*]

SIR G. : [*Seeing Meg still standing on the parapet*] What ! Are
you still up there ?

MEG : I'm—I'm scared to jump !

[*Meg half-jumps, half-falls and Willie free of his own
ropes springs forward and catches her*]

Oh, Willie !

WILLIE : Are you all right, Meg ?

MEG : Aye, thank you, lad. You just caught me in time.

WILLIE : It's me should be thanking you, lass. You saved
my life.

MEG : Och, my father wasn't in earnest. He was just
trying to frighten us.

WILLIE : That for a story ! Were you in earnest about
the jumping, lass ?

MEG : Aye, Willie, I was. [*She turns away from him and goes
to the corner of the battlements. He follows her*]

SIR G. : Here they come with Andra. Is it not like Andra
to let me down like this ?

GRIZEL : It's the very best thing that could have happened !

[*Grizel exits and Sir G. follows her as far as the door
where he turns*]

SIR G. : [*To Willie*] Are you coming ?

WILLIE : I'll be with you the now.

SIR G. : Well, hurry up ! [*Exits*]

MEG : I suppose this is the end, Willie ?

WILLIE : Aye, I suppose it is. Eh, but it's grand to be a
free man again. [*He stretches himself luxuriantly*]

MEG : I'm glad you're pleased, Willie.

WILLIE : Are you not pleased, Meg ?

MEG : I'm pleased for you, Willie. [*She has been half-turned
away from him during these speeches. Now she puts one hand*

over her mouth and turns to him with the other outheld] Farewell, my braw lad! Don't think too hardly of me.

WILLIE: [*Ignoring her proffered hand*] What are you holding your hand like that for?

MEG: You ken why, Willie.

WILLIE: Take it down.

MEG: No, Willie. It's better this way. If you have your last look of me like this maybe you'll mind the eyes and forget the rest.

WILLIE: Take down your hand!

MEG: Aye, Willie. [*Her hand drops but her head droops too. She cannot look at him. He puts a hand under her chin and raises her face and kisses her*]

MEG: Willie! (*She steps away from him with her face transfigured by joy*] Oh, Willie, does that mean . . .

WILLIE: Aye, seeing we're this far I think we may as well go on with it. Come on, lass! Let's go down and see your father. But mind, Meg! We've got to get the wee black bull with the tocher!

MEG: Oh, Willie!

[*They run out arm in arm, and Wattie, looking after them, scratches his towsled head*]

WATTIE: Well, what do you think of that?

THOMAS: [*Bitterly*] I'm past thinking of anything, Wattie. [*He tears up the MS. of his ballad and scatters the pieces*]

WATTIE: Is that your ballad you're tearing up?

THOMAS: I'm done with ballads, and I'm done with Elibank. This is the last that you'll see of me here.

WATTIE: Why! Where are you off to now, Thomas?

THOMAS: To Elfland, Wattie, to Elfland—the only place for a poet! And I wish I had never left it.

94

WATTIE : [*Half seating himself on the gibbet platform*] Thomas, what's it like there? You never told us.

THOMAS : [*His face lighting up*] Elfland? It's hard to describe it to you, Wattie. You see there's nothing in this world that you can right compare it to . . . unless . . . well, you ken how the world looks when you're full, but not too full?

WATTIE : That's heaven you're speaking about!

THOMAS : Oh no, heaven's different. That's the Elfland, Wattie—all the pleasures of intoxication with never a morning after.

WATTIE : It sounds more like heaven than ever! [*Hesitantly and not very hopefully*] Thomas, I suppose you couldn't take me along with you?

THOMAS : No, Wattie. I'm sorry. Unless the Queen o' Elfland comes for you herself, there's no road to yon place.

WATTIE : Oh well, there was no harm in asking! [*He lets the hammer he has picked up again fall with a thud on the platform and rises*] I'd better get down now.

THOMAS : Aye, aye, Wattie.

> [*Wattie goes out left and Thomas is left alone. The light fades and the battlements change back to the moonlit woods where Thomas's adventures began*]

THOMAS : And now I wonder if she'll come for me? Maybe she'll not be so keen since I made such a hash of the ballad! Losh! What if she doesn't come and I have to stay on here with the curse on me—neither an honest burgher of the town of sense nor a freeman of the world of imagination! [*Agitated*] lady! Are you there, lady? It's me—Thomas. Lady! Where are you, lady?

[*The Lady in Green appears*]

THE L.I.G.: Well, Thomas?

THOMAS: [*Wheeling round*] Lady! Oh, but I'm glad to see you. I should never have left you. [*He takes a step towards her but she draws back*]

THE L.I.G.: So you've learned that much have you? Well, that's something gained. Well, where's the fine ballad you were to bring me?

THOMAS: [*Downcast*] I tore it up. It wouldn't work out the way I wanted it.

THE L.I.G.: Oh! It's not you who've lost the art of making them, maybe?

THOMAS: [*Indignant*] Me? I'm the best ba—— Na! It was Willie Scott that let me down. Him and the awful curse you put on me. If it hadn't been for that, with a touch here and a touch there I'd a made . . . ach, but you were right, lady. This is no world for a poet— especially when he's cursed with a tongue that's forbid to lie.

THE L.I.G.: [*Softening*] Never mind, Thomas. Cheer up! There's aye me—and Elfland. [*She takes his hand*]

THOMAS: Aye, there's aye that. [*He looks back at the world he has come from*] Ach! To hell with the world! Come on, lady, let's go.

THE L.I.G.: [*As they go into the trees*] Mind you, Thomas, it never was . . .

THOMAS: Never was what?

THE L.I.G.: A world for a poet . . .

THE END OF THE PLAY

THE WORLD'S WONDER

A Phantasy

For
GENEVIEVE

CHARACTERS

MICHAEL SCOTT	*a wizard*
THE FALSE SCOTT	*an impostor*
LAZARUS	*a young man of inquiring mind*
PROVOST SIR DAVIE PEEBLES	*a rogue*
LIZZIE, THE PROVOST'S WIFE	*a termagant*
THE LAIRD OF CLARTYDYKES	*a fool*
JEANNIE	*a country lassie*
JOCK	*a shepherd laddie*
THE BELLMAN-BAILIE	*another rogue*
WILLIE	*a devil*
THE DANCING BEAR	*a comedian*
THE PRIEST	*an accomplice*
THE VEGETABLE VENDOR	*a country-woman*
THE BEAR-LEADER	*the bear-led*
AN EXCITED MAN	*a man excited*
THE STONE MAN	*a " familiar "*
THE VEGETABLE MAN	*another*
SUMMER	*a dancer*
CAPTAIN OF THE GUARD	*a pawn of Sir Davie's*

CITIZENS OF DUBBITY

First produced by the Glasgow Citizens Theatre at the Royal Princess's Theatre, Glasgow, May 11, 1953.

MICHAEL SCOTT	Andrew Keir
THE FALSE SCOTT	Lea Ashton
LAZARUS	Roddy MacMillan
PROVOST SIR DAVIE PEEBLES	James Gibson
THE LAIRD O' CLARTYDYKES	Michael Elder
JEANNIE	Iris Russell
JOCK	James Gilbert
THE BELLMAN-BAILIE	Paul Curran
THE PROVOST'S WIFE	Madeleine Christie
THE BEAR-LEADER	Robert Grayson
THE DANCING BEAR	Mary Wylie
THE STOOKY MAN	Alistair Wilson
VEGETABLE MAN	Peter Stuart Smith
THE VEGETABLE WIFE	Marillyn Gray
WILLIE	Daniel Caldwell
THE PRIEST	Robert Grayson
AN EXCITED MAN	Daniel Caldwell
CAPTAIN OF THE GUARD	Peter Stuart Smith

Producer : Peter Potter

First produced in England at the Questors' Theatre, Ealing, January 8, 1955.

Producer : Pamela Richards

ACT ONE

ACT TWO

ACT THREE

ACT I

SCENE ONE

*The Market Place of the Burgh of Dubbity in Tweedsdale,
Scotland, at the end of the Middle Ages. In the middle of the
square is the Market Cross. On the left is the Church and a
statue of a bygone Provost, sculptured standing at a stone desk
reading a huge stone book. Back, on a blunted corner, with streets
running off to left and right of it, stands the house of Sir David
Peebles, the present Provost. On the right is a row of houses and
shops, a market stall for the sale of vegetables, and the Burgh
Pillory. The month is March, the hour midnight, a huge full
golden moon shines down over the roof-tops, and two windows in
the Provost's house are lighted, one, right of the door, on the
ground floor, the other left of the door, on the upper flat. Jock, a
shaggy-headed young man in the dress of a shepherd, steals into
the Place and takes a step or two towards the Provost's house,
then hearing the Bailie-Bellman (now on watch) approaching,
hurriedly takes cover behind the statue. The Bailie-Bellman,
carrying a lantern, walks pompously across the Place.*

BELLMAN : Twelve o'clock and a full moon shining ! [*He
yawns hugely and gives a half-turn to his rattle*] Twelve o' the
clock—and a fine night for them that can sleep !
> [*The Bailie-Bellman exits and Jock comes out from cover
> and tiptoes across the Place till he stands beneath the
> lighted window of the second floor of the Provost's house*]

9

JOCK : [*Low*] Jeannie !

> [*There is no answer and stooping he finds a pebble and throws it at the window*]

  Hi ! Jeannie.

> [*This time he is successful, Jeannie appears at the window, pushes it open and leans out*]

JEANNIE : [*Low*] Who's there ?

JOCK : [*Low*] It's me, Jeannie.

JEANNIE : [*Lower and frightened*] Oh Jock, you shouldn't have come. You know what the Provost said !

JOCK : [*Low*] I had to come, Jeannie. I had to see you ! Can you come down ?

JEANNIE : [*Low*] Well . . . oh, all right. But just for a minute. And keep away from the window in case they see you.

JOCK : [*Low*] All right, Jeannie.

> [*Jeannie closes the window and Jock takes cover by the Cross. After a moment the door of the Provost's house is opened a slit and Jeannie slips out. She comes out into the moonlight and looks about for Jock*]

JEANNIE : Jock ?

JOCK : [*Stepping clear of Cross*] I'm here, Jeannie.

> [*Jeannie runs to him and they cling together*]

JEANNIE : Oh, Jock !

JOCK : Oh, Jeannie !

> [*They kiss*]

  Is the wedding still on ?

JEANNIE : [*All her joy vanished*] Aye, so they say, Jock. Unless something happens to put off the ceremony, by this time the morn I'll be wed to the Laird o' Clartydykes. It's a fearful thought.

JOCK: It is indeed . . . Jeannie, could we no just run for it?

JEANNIE: Aye, but run where?

JOCK: Aye, that's the rub, where in the world could we run to where they wouldn't find us? Oh Jeannie! Jeannie! I wonder if ever true lovers before have suffered like this?

JEANNIE: Who ever loved like us, Jock?

JOCK: Aye, that's true too, when you think of it. We and our situation are without a precedent. You could near make a play on us.

JEANNIE: It would be too sad, Jock. Plays have happy endings and I can't see the faintest glimmer of hope of a happy ending to our love-story. . . . Oh Jock, I think I'll die if I lose you. I'm so fond of you.

JOCK: And me of you, Jeannie.

[*They cling together in another kiss. The Bailie-Bellman returns*]

BELLMAN: By Twel—— [*He sees Jock and Jeannie and breaking off his cry rushes over to them with upraised lantern*] Here! What's this? What's this? Well, I'll be jiggered! If it's not the Provost's daughter and Jock the Shepherd! [*Setting down lantern and dragging them apart*] Hi! Break it up! Break it up! Kissing at crosses is strictly prohibited!

JOCK: [*Aghast*] The Bailie-Bellman!

JEANNIE: [*Clinging to him*] Oh, Jock!

BELLMAN: [*To Jeannie*] And you to be married the morn, too! Are you not ashamed? [*Shouting to house*] Hi! Provost! Lizzie! Come and see what I've here!

[*There is a noise in the Provost's house and the door is*

*flung open and the Provost armed with a blunderbuss,
and Lizzie, his wife, carrying a lantern and a poker,
appear*]

PROVOST: [*Alarmed*] What's up, Bailie? Have they found
us out?

LIZZIE: [*Alarmed*] Are they coming to burn the house?

BELLMAN: No, no, it's not that. But see who I've
apprehended!

[*He lifts his lantern and shines it on the lovers*]

I caught them red-lippèd in the act of kissing this very
minute.

PROVOST: [*Amazed*] Jeannie and Jock! Well, I'll be
flabbergasted!

LIZZIE: [*To Provost*] I told you to lock her in! [*To Jeannie,
threatening her with the poker*] You ill-got randy! If I'd
my way I'd teach you the word obedience with the
weight of this poker!

PROVOST: Wheest! Lizzie, wheest! We don't want to
waken the neighbours.

The last thing we want the night is a public scandal.

The Laird knows nothing of Jock and until Jean's
wedding——

JEANNIE: [*Passionately*] I'll not be wed to the Laird. I
hate him!

PROVOST: You'll wed who I choose, my lass. Dear sake!
I'm your father amn't I, besides the Provost?

LIZZIE: I know what——

PROVOST: Now, Liz, hold your tongue! Let me handle
this situation.

The matter's delicate. It needs politic handling.

Now first for the shepherd here. I've told you before
   Jock——
Three times at least!—to keep away from my daughter.
She's not for the likes of you. Now here's final warning.
If you put as much as a foot in the bounds of Dubbity
Between this warning and the hour of our Jeannie's
   wedding,
I'll have you jailed for breaching the peace of my mind,
Obstructing my plans, and aye! take note now, Bailie,
For the crime of arson!

BELLMAN: [*Puzzled*] Did you say arson?

PROVOST: Arson I said. I'm fair in a blaze this minute!
   And now you, Jeannie.

JEANNIE: [*Fearfully*] Aye, Provost?

PROVOST: Away to your room you graceless, undutiful
   daughter, before you get moon-struck!

JEANNIE: [*Staring*] Moon-struck?

PROVOST: Moon-struck or worse—bespelled by some witch
   or warlock
Broom-sticking eastwards for the Law of Berwick
The air's fair thick with them. Take her in now, Liz.

LIZZIE: Come on, you hussy!

JEANNIE: [*Resisting her*] Oh, Jock! I believe, I really
   believe I can see it!

JOCK: [*Straining towards her against the grasp of the Bellman*]
   See what, Jeannie?

JEANNIE: [*Smiling*] The faintest glimmer of hope of a
   happy ending.

LIZZIE: [*Pushing her*] Will you come, you minx, you!

JEANNIE: I'm coming. Farewell, Jock, and don't despair.

JOCK: Farewell, Jeannie.

LIZZIE : [*Leading Jeannie off*] Oh, I'd like to batter you !

PROVOST : [*Staring after them*]

Dear me ! I believe she's a touch of the moon already ! You'll see him out of the town ?

BELLMAN : Trust me, Sir Davie.

PROVOST : Right ! I'll get in then.

[*Rushing after Lizzie and Jeannie*]

Now careful there, Lizzie woman !

Don't you put marks on her where the Laird can see them !

   [*He exits into the house after Jeannie and Lizzie*]

BELLMAN : Come on you. Off you go !

JOCK : What did she mean about a happy ending ?

BELLMAN : [*Pushing him on*] How should I know and anyway what does it matter ?

You'll not be in it ! Get on now and mind what the Provost told you.

It's lucky for you you're not on your road to jail !

   [*Jock and the Bellman vanish round the corner of the church and the market place is now empty. The light in Jeannie's window dims as a blind is pulled down sharply. Lizzie's shadow threatening Jeannie with the poker appears on it, then we see Lizzie lift a candle and blow. As the candle goes out the window blacks out. A pause. The window on the first floor blacks out. A pause. The moon blacks out. Dubbity sleeps*]

SCENE TWO

The Market Place, late in the afternoon, four days later. The place is bustling with Dubbities, men, women and children, and the pillory has now an occupant, Lazarus, a young man of inquiring disposition, who, as a notice nailed to a nearby post informs the public, is suffering punishment " For asking questions and cheeking the Provost." Round the prisoner's feet are the bruised vegetables and broken eggs which have been thrown at him and nearby a fat vegetable wife, her stall open and her wares displayed, is crying for custom. The citizens of Dubbity, however, have tired of baiting Lazarus, and are now gathered about an old bear which is jigging to a penny whistle blown by the bear-leader, in front of the Provost's house. Though it is a greyish day the bright costumes of the Dubbities make the scene a colourful one.

VEGETABLE WOMAN: Fine leeks! Fine onions! Come and buy! Come and buy! Bad eggs for throwing! Three shots a groat! Bad eggs for throwing! Three shots a groat! What do you lack? Fine leeks! Fine onions! What do you lack?

> [*Suddenly the church bells begin to ring. The bear-leader stops piping, the stall-holder crying, the bear dancing and everybody—including Lazarus, so far as he is able, and the bear, which, to get a better view drags the bear-leader after it by its chain to the middle of the square—looks up the street leading off back left of the church at the corner of which an excited man appears*]

15

EXCITED MAN: He's coming, folks! Tell the Provost somebody.

> [*The excited man rushes off the way he has come. Two citizens rush up the steps to knock on the door of the Provost's house and are almost knocked over by the Provost and Bellman rushing out, the Provost dragging on his scarlet gown as he runs, the Bellman ringing his bell*]

PROVOST: Out of the way there! Clear the roads, folk!

> [*But there is no need for these instructions. Everyone else in the square except Lazarus (who can't) and including the bear—dragging its leader after it on the chain—has dashed off after the excited man shouting as they go*]

TOWNSFOLK: It's the warlock coming! Now we'll see something! They say he's marvellous!

> [*The Provost and Bellman hurry after the others and the square is empty except for Lazarus, when from a road coming into the square from the opposite direction there enters Michael Scott, an elderly gentleman with a long white beard, a very upright carriage. Scott is dressed all in black. On his back, wrapped in a black velvet cloth, he carries a rectangular object about the size and shape of a wardrobe mirror. In his hand is a long black staff, and slung over his shoulder is a bulging black bag. He walks into the middle of the square, gazing around him, sees Lazarus and is about to speak to him, but the clamour of the bells is very loud and instead he looks up at the bell-tower and raises his wand*]

MICHAEL: Wheest!

> [*The bells stop immediately and Michael is again on the point of speaking when one small rather tinny bell renews its tinkling*]

16

MICHAEL: Did you hear me speak, you brazen jangler?
Stop when you're told or by my books I'll blast you!
> [*The bell stops abruptly, gives a small tinkle, then, as if gaining courage, rings on faster, louder*]

MICHAEL: [*Without animosity*] Blast you!
> [*There is an explosion in the bell-tower and the bell, blasted, is heard tinkling down inside the structure*]

[*To tower*] That's stopped her capers!

[*Crooking a finger at Lazarus*]

Come forth, Lazarus!

LAZARUS: [*Longingly*] I wish I could, sir.

MICHAEL: You can! You must! Come here, I said!

LAZARUS: I tell——
> [*Before he can protest any more the pillory falls to pieces and he pitches forward on his hands and knees. Still kneeling he looks back first at the broken pillory, then up at Michael*]

Did you do that, sir?

MICHAEL: [*Carelessly*] Oh aye! That's easy. But let bird fly!

[*He pokes Lazarus with his wand*]

Tell me, my lad, wherefor the choiring bells?

Where's all the folk?—the Provost? Bailie-Bellman?

Where's the goodwives? where's all the scampering bairns?

Between the South Gate and the Market Place here
Barring yourself I've met not a living body!
I've seen more stir of life in Yarrow churchyard
At dark of midnight than I've wakened here!
What drove them out? You'd think the old Black Death
Or the yellow Leprosy had ta'en up lodgings.

[*Pokes him again*]

Get up you lump! Compose yourself! Come! Come!
[*Lazarus gets up*]

Speak up! Speak out! You've no cause to be dumb.
What's ta'en the place? What's made it such a desert?
Where's all the citizens of Dubbity?

LAZARUS: [*His knees knocking*]

If you p-please, Your Honour, they've all g-gone out to
welcome the g-great warlock!

MICHAEL: [*To himself*] That's me, of course. There's but
one warlock great!

And yet it's queer. It's out of all measure queer!
It wasn't my intent to supper here!
It's not four hours back that the smell of wood-smoke
And a tinkling stream-song put Tweeddale in mind
Setting my shoes,—clean contrary to my will!—
Wearing this way. [*To Lazarus*]

What's he like this warlock?

LAZARUS: If it please Your Honour, he's as like

Your Honour, as two branches on the one tree, two
boughs on the one branch, two twigs on the one
bough, two——

MICHAEL: Hold on! Rein up! I get your general drift.

You think, you say, you see some slight resemblance
'Twixt him and me?

LAZARUS: A most notable resemblance—if it please

Your Honour! A most marvellous and extraordinary
resemblance. And yet . . .

MICHAEL: And yet?

LAZARUS: Now that I see you close I believe the other
was more—[*Michael looks threatening*]

I mean less !—awe-inspiring !

MICHAEL : Aye, that's more like it ! But tell me this now.
This man like me—but not just so awe-inspiring—
When was he last in Dubbity ?

LAZARUS : T-two days back—if it please Your Wizardship.

MICHAEL : [*Musing*] Two days you say ? Two days ?

LAZARUS : That's right, Your Honour.

MICHAEL : Then it wasn't me that the Dubbities expected !
Two days back I was on the Kelvinside
Hunting the fairies ! By my books I swear
I've not touched Dubbity in fifty year !
There's some dark mystery in this town it's plain.
This Man you speak of. Do you know his name ?

LAZARUS : Oh aye, he's Michael Scott.

MICHAEL : [*Exploding*] He's Michael *what* ?
[*Lazarus cringes away*]

LAZARUS : That's what he said, sir : Michael Scott.

MICHAEL : By hell's black cauldrons ! If you give me
sauce, lad,
I'll turn you goose and cook and eat you with it !
I'm Michael Scott.
[*He lifts wand threateningly and Lazarus cringes again*]

LAZARUS : I believe you, sir. I believe you !
[*Michael relaxes*]
I said you were more awe-inspiring didn't I ?
But Your Worship's Honour, if this man's not you—
I mean, not whom he says he is. Who is he then ?

MICHAEL : [*Grimly*] That we'll find out ! And then this
damned impostor
We'll teach a lesson that he'll not forget
In a month of Sundays !

To steal my name! To steal my honourable name!
By Merlin's cap and Nostrodamus's chart!
I'll make him smart for it! But tell me quick now
What brings the faker into Dubbity?

LAZARUS: The proclamation, Your Honour. Did you not
hear of it?

MICHAEL: I take no heed of village gossip. What proclamation?

LAZARUS: The one about Jeannie Peebles—the Provost's
daughter.

It was cried not long past by the Bellman-Bailie.

[*The Bellman-Bailie's bell sounds and the Bellman-Bailie
walks in pompously from the right and takes up a stance
on the steps of the Provost's house*]

BELLMAN: Oyeh! Oyeh! Oyeh!
Hearken to me you citizens of Dubbity!
Attend! Put by your work! Prick up your ears!
Give full attention to this proclamation.
Jeannie, the Provost's daughter's been bespelled
Cast by enchantment in a waking dream
On her wedding morn. For four days now she's been
More like a painted image than a maid,
Nor priests with bells and books, nor doctor's nostrums—
Hot plasters, poultices and burnt feathers
Can shift and rid her of this burry magic
So fast it sticks! Wherefore, her worthy father,
Sir David Peebles, Provost of Dubbity town,
Being sore troubled by the great expense
Caused by the postponed wedding, bids me say,
If any witch or warlock, well-disposed
To folk in Dubbity should hear this cry,

And would by counter magic lift the spell—
Rich their reward! He'll give a purse of gold
And raise them freemen of our noble city!

    [He rings the bell again and walks off down the left-hand
    street, renewing his cry which is heard fading into distance]

Oyeh! Oyeh! Oyeh! etc.

MICHAEL: And this impostor answered to that cry
Under my name?

LAZARUS: That's right, Your Honour.

    [The sound of the townsfolk returning is heard in the distance]

                          But look! See there, sir,
Here he comes now in arms with Provost Peebles
With half the townsfolk trooping at their heels!
Man, but he's like—he's like you as your brother!

    [Michael steps out to see]

MICHAEL: He's like my image in a looking glass
If the glass were crooked! Quick! Come behind this
    stall

    [He hurries Lazarus behind vegetable stall]

I'll teach this cheating juggler to play me
Or by the pale cheek of the waning moon,
I'll burn my wand!

*[On the last word Michael bobs down under cover and a moment
later Provost Peebles and the False Scott, with the townsfolk,
enter the square. The Provost and the False Scott mount the
steps of the Provost's house out of which to join them comes
Lizzie, the Provost's wife; the Dubbities gather below
cheering. The dancing bear not being able to cheer, dances]*

TOWNSFOLK: Hurrah for the warlock! Long live the
wizard! Show us some tricks, mister!

[*The bellman rings his bell*]

BELLMAN: Wheest there! Wheest! Silence for Sir Davie Peebles, Hereditary Provost of the town of Dubbity!

[*Silence is obtained*]

PROVOST: [*Blowing his nose loudly*] Thank you! Thank you! We're much obliged to you, friends, much obliged.

[*He takes oratorical stance*]

Fellow townsfolk of the good town of Dubbity! We are met here on a most happy—I mean a most *unhappy* occasion. My daughter Jeannie, as you all know— [*with chuckle and nudging to Bellman*]—or my good friend the Bellman has been pouching the shillings for nothing!—

VEGETABLE WOMAN: [*Throwing in*] That wouldn't surprise us! [*laughter*]

PROVOST: [*Holding up hand*] . . . my daughter Jeannie, as I was about to say, has, if I may so express myself, had the misfortune to be ill-looked. [*Murmur of sympathy*] About ten days back as you'll maybe remember—I can tell you I'll not forget that day in a hurry!—Jeannie was, as you all know, to be married to that rich—I mean to that noble—though his pockets are well-lined too and I'm sure none of us here think the worse of him for that! —I'm sure I don't!—to that most, well, let's say it right out!—to that most rich and noble nobleman, that good friend of Dubbity, the Laird of Clartydykes. . . .

TOWNSFOLK: [*Angrily*] Away with him!

Boo!

Put him in the pond!

Up with the townsfolk and herds and down with the Clartydykes!

[*Out of the midst of the anti-Laird demonstration a song arises in which all the townsfolk join and during which the bear dances around joyously and the Bellman unavailingly rings his bell*]

TOWNSFOLK : [*Singing*]

      Up with the burghers o' Dubbity !
      Up with the cobblers and herds !
      Hi up with the plain woollen bonnets
      And down with the Clartydykes Lairds !
      Who spoiled the good town of its commons ?
      Who robbed us with papers and swords ?
      Who sold us for money and powers ?
      To hell with the Clartydyke Lords !

BELLMAN : [*Shouting above uproar*] Wheest ! Hold your tongue there or I'll put the lot of you in jail !

[*The uproar subsides*]

Carry on, Provost !

PROVOST : [*Blowing his nose*] Aye, aye, that's all right. That's all right. [*Blows his nose like a trumpet*] As I was saying when I was interrupted by some ruffians—no honest Dubbities I'm sure !—and by the by, in case there's any more of it I'll just remind you now that amongst the other amenities of this burgh we have a Town Jail !— Aye ! [*Blows nose again*] However, to continue. As I was saying when I was interrupted just now, my daughter Jeannie, on the very morning of her wedding, had the misfortune to be ill-looked by some damned witch or warlock. [*Chuckling and patting the False Scott's shoulder*] Not meaning you, friend, not meaning you !—and the whole thing—and mark you these things aren't put on for nothing !—the whole thing had to be put off. [*Blows*

nose] Well, well, friends, I'll say no more about that.
What I want to say now is . . . [*Largely*] it's an ill-wind
that blows nobody good ! [*Cheers from crowd*] What's my
misfortune is Dubbity's fortune ! [*Cheers*] Since . . .
since fellow burghers, it has brought into our midst,
the gentleman now standing beside me. . . . [*He puts
a hand on the False Scott's shoulder and the townsfolk cheer*]
. . . a warlock whose name and fame are well-known to
the youngest amongst you ; a man, if I may venture to
say it, in his own profession, out of the very top drawer !
[*More cheers*] Thank you ! Thank you ! And now, fellow-
Dubbities—that's quite enough for me so I'll close up
now by asking our honoured guest, whose name I need
hardly mention—[*in whisper to Bellman*] What the devil
is his name ?

BELLMAN : [*Behind hand*] Scott. Michael Scott.

PROVOST : Oh aye ! Whose name—as I was about to say
when the Bellman interrupted me with some important
Town business—is . . . Mister Michael Scott !—[*Cheering
is starting again but he silences it*] to say a word to you
before we go into the house for a bite and a sup. Mister
Michael Scott !

> [*The Dubbities cheer loudly and while they do so the
> Provost goes down a step leaving the centre to the False
> Scott who addresses the crowd in a very affected voice.
> Early in his speech the real Michael, rising unobserved
> from behind the stall, makes passes towards the crowd
> with his hands and mutters what is presumably a spell,
> then ducks down again*]

FALSE SCOTT : Good people of Dubbity, may A first of all
thenk you for the very kaind reception you have accorded

24

me to-day. [*Applause*] Your hereditary Provost, Sir
Davie—if a friend of so small acquaintance can presume
to call him Sir Davie?

[*The Provost, head on one side, nods and beams*]

PROVOST: Aye, surely! Surely!

FALSE SCOTT: Thank you, Sir Davie. Your worshipful
Provost, Sir Davie here, has, A must say, made some
haighly complimentary remarks about mai accomplish-
ments in the realm of witchery, warlockery or as it is
more properly called at St. Endrews University where
I spent mainy heppy years, the airt of sorcery, conjuring
or legerdemain . . .

MICHAEL: [*Bobbing up*] You're a damned liar! [*Bobs down*]

[*There is a general stir. The Bellman rings his bell*]

BELLMAN: Silence there! Any more interruptions like
that and l'll clear the street! Carry on, sir.

FALSE SCOTT: A shall disregard thet interruption. To
continue, A was about to say, that if I were to claim
A had inherited the sword of Paracelsus, the books of
Faustus and the cap of the great Merlin, there are no
doubt scoffers among you who would say—

PROVOST: [*Suddenly*] Cock-a-doodle-doo!

[*While the crowd roars with laughter and Michael and
Lazarus behind the stall are in great glee, the Provost,
much embarrassed claps his hand to his mouth*]

FALSE SCOTT: Really, Mr. Provost!

PROVOST: [*Placatingly*] I—I'm right sorry, Your Wizardship.
I—I don't know what came over me. [*To crowd, bluster-
ingly*] Now you behave yourselves down there! Carry
on, Mr. Scott.

FALSE SCOTT: Are you quate sure . . .?

PROVOST: Aye, aye. I'm all right now. Carry on, sir.

FALSE SCOTT: Very well. [*Snaps his fingers*] Tk! A have quaite lost the thread of my discourse.

PROVOST: [*Anxious to make amends*] If I remember right, Mister Scott, you broke off just at the words——

BELLMAN: [*Catching it*] Cock-a-doodle-doo!

> [*Amid more laughter the Provost rushes up to the Bellman and catching him by the arm shakes him angrily*]

PROVOST: Stop it! Stop it! Stop it or I'll crown you!

> [*But the Bellman shakes himself free and goes strutting about the square and stretching his neck like a cock and crowing loudly*]

BELLMAN: Cock-a-doodle-doo!

PROVOST: He's off his head! Oh Lord! Here's another of them caught it!

> [*This time it is the vegetable woman who has caught the infection and while the Bellman struts and crows she rushes about the square clucking like a hen*]

VEG. WOMAN: Oh! took-took-took-took-took! Oh! took-took-took-took-took!

BELLMAN: [*Strutting up to Provost*] Cock-a-doodle-doo!

> [*He makes a pecking jump at the Provost and the Provost jumps back in the same fashion*]

PROVOST: [*Catching it again*] Cock-a-doodle-doo!

> [*He and the Bellman jump about pecking at each other and crowing and one by one the other Dubbities catch the infection. The men crow and jump. The women run about clucking. Finally even the bear catches it and sitting down in the middle of the square lifts its head and crows*]

THE BEAR: Cock-a-doodle-doo!

> [*The only person out on the square unaffected by the spell*

*is the False Scott who rushes about catching at one person
after another crying :*]

FALSE SCOTT : Stop it ! Stop it !

[*But the madness goes on until the real Michael and
Lazarus come out from behind the stall. They stand for
a moment regarding the scene with much amazement, then
Michael raises his wand*]

MICHAEL : Stop !

[*At the word everybody in the square, including the False
Scott (and the bear), freeze in whatever attitude they have
been caught in. A pause. Michael drops his wand*]

All right. You can come to now . . .

[*The Dubbities return to life. They look at each other,
puzzled at what has been happening to them*]

BELLMAN : What happened ? [*Sees the real Michael*] Oh !
Lord ! There's two of them now !

PROVOST : What ?   What ?   The   Lord   preserve   us !
Who's this ?

[*The crowd, murmuring, draws back from Michael*]

MICHAEL : [*Stepping forward*] A warlock, and a real one !
Provost Peebles !

I charge that faker by the Town House steps there
With vain pretending to my name and fame !
I'm Michael Scott !

PROVOST : [*Nervously*] Can this be true ?

FALSE SCOTT : No, it's not true ! Don't heed him,
Provost.

It's him that's the impostor here. I'm Michael Scott.

MICHAEL : Man, Provost, will you just take a look at us !
Is it not clear as day is clear from night
Which is the real Scott and which the faker ?

PROVOST: T-tell you the truth, sirs, I can't see a hairs-breadth of difference between the two of you. C-can you, Bellman?

BELLMAN: [*Studying them*] No. Unless maybe that one [*pointing at Michael*] is more like the other one than the other's like him?

PROVOST: [*Considering it*] Do you think so? No, I can't agree with you. To my mind if anything, it's the other way round.

FALSE SCOTT: Maight A point out Sir Davie, A was here first so A have the prior claim. However, if you want my credentials . . . [*Snaps his fingers and there is a clap of thunder and flash of lightning*] I hope that convinces you!

> [*The Townsfolk shrink back at the thunderclap but Michael laughs*]

MICHAEL: Ha! When Michael Scott's in town he knocks louder than that! [*He snaps his fingers*]

> [*Several crashes of thunder and brilliant lightning*]

Well, Provost, does that help you to make up your mind?

PROVOST: [*In difficulties*] I—I can see that you're both most prussient warlocks, sirs, but which is the true Scott and which the false, well, I would hardly dare to commit myself. Could you—could you not settle it between yourselves, sirs?

MICHAEL: Aye, that we could, if this impostor dared.

FALSE SCOTT: You mean a duel?

MICHAEL: I do!

FALSE SCOTT: A've no objection.

The usual programme and the Camelot rules?

MICHAEL: That suits me fine! We fight three rounds
and who

Has best of three's the one true Scott. Agreed?

FALSE SCOTT: Agreed! Stand back, you folk, I need more
room,

Here on the ground to draw my magic pentagon.

[*He marks out the pentagon with the point of his wand*]

MICHAEL: Here, Lazarus. Hold this bag while I draw
mine. [*Michael has already unstrapped the mirror. Now he
hands the bag to Lazarus and sketches out the pentagon in a
careless sort of way. The figures are completed at the same time
and the two warlocks straighten themselves together*] All set?

FALSE SCOTT: Oh aye. A'm ready.

MICHAEL: Then let the Bellman ring and try your hand,

First at the pleasing art of transformations.

Then I'll try mine and let the Dubbities judge

Which of the two is the most skilled magician,

For he most skilled is passed all chance and doubt

True Michael Scott. Agreed?

FALSE SCOTT: Agreed! [*to Townsfolk*] And now prepare to
look on marvels!

The year's at March. The Spring is half-way here,

But there's a demon of the mist and snow

Bound bai my word! Hark, Demon, and obey!

[*He raises his wand*]

By the bare fields and the bare black trees!

By the howling tempest and the dog-toothed seas!

By rain and rain-rot! By the scudding sleet!

By muddy highways and the weary street!

By coughs and sneezes and a dripping nose!

By cold! By hunger! And by ragged clothes!

By the lost sheep-flock in the drift deep-buried !
By the dead shepherd that the foxes worried !
By death ! By desolation ! want ! and woe !
I conjure Winter !

> [*It grows dark. The wind whistles dismally then rises to a howling gale. It begins to snow heavily*]

TOWNSFOLK : Oooooh !

> [*The townsfolk turn up their collars, shiver, stamp, sneeze and cough. At last the snow thins out, the wind dies down, the light becomes normal. The Dubbities applaud, but not too enthusiastically*]

BELLMAN : Ach ! That was terrible. [*To Michael*] Can you better it, sir ?

MICHAEL : [*Easily*] Oh aye ! I think so. It would be a poor magician
That could not summon up power enough to charm
Out of a Scots March sky a flutter of snow.
Hold on a wee and I'll show you a trick worth ten of it.
[*Lifts wand and winks at crowd*]
I'll make it Summer !
[*Short pause*]
By a red rose bud and a white rose flowering !
By two fond lovers in a hedge-nook cowering !
By swallows twittering and the cuckoo's bawling !
By frogs hoarse croaking and the bat's high calling !
By cows bent homewards with their udders swinging !
By buzzing bee-swarms and the thrush's singing !
By laddies bathing in the low warm pools
Their thoughts on all things but the lear of schools !
By old folk sunning in the green kale patches !
And green shoots spouting on the old brown thatches !

By gold-eyed daisies and blue summer skies
By hell-born midges and bright butterflies
By the long days, and by the nights so clear !
By the good grain swelling in the rustling ear !
By the blessèd sun ! By the moon of dreams !
June's witched moon ! By strawberries and cream !
    I conjure Summer !

[*At this invocation the sky turns blue ; the sun shines with exaggerated brilliance ; a multitude of birds begin singing*]

TOWNSFOLK : Aaaaaaah !

[*Some take off their jackets ; others fan themselves and mop their brows. Suddenly faint music is heard and the nymph of Summer, dancing in a comic fashion weaves her way across the square scattering flowers as she goes. As she passes near Lazarus he puts his fingers into his mouth and whistles after her like a corner boy. Michael, scandalised catches him by the arm*]

MICHAEL : Behave yourself, Lazarus !

[*As the nymph exits Michael makes a pass with his wand, the music and birdsong fade and the lights return to normal. The Dubbities applaud enthusiastically*].

Well, folks, what's the verdict ?

Which do you like best ? Summer or winter ?

TOWNSFOLK : Summer ! Summer ! Give us more summer !

FALSE SCOTT : Bah !

MICHAEL : First point to us, Lazarus ! Mark it up ! Mark it up !

[*Lazarus looks for something to mark it up on and finally tears down the notices from the pillory board revealing a black board beneath. At the top, on one side, he writes ' Real Scott ' and on the other ' False Scott.' He makes a 1 under False Scott then hastily rubs it out and puts it in the other column. The Bellman rings his bell.*

BELLMAN : The first round goes to the warlock on my left. Take your places for Round Two, gentlemen—and by the by, what is it to be this time ?

FALSE SCOTT : [*Snappily*] Curses, blastings, and maledictions!

BELLMAN : [*Affronted*] There's no need to swear at a civil question, sir !

FALSE SCOTT : A'm not swearing, you fool ! A'm telling you what the next round will be !

MICHAEL : It's all right, Bellman. It's the usual order.

BELLMAN : Oh ? Oh well, have it your own way. [*Rings bell*] Round Two—Curses, Blastings, and——

PROVOST : [*Coming forward, scratching his ear*] Just a minute, there. If Your Warlockries'll forgive me, I'm just a shade worried about this round. Curses, blastings and the like are perilous things to be flying around loose if you follow me, and as the Provost of Dubbity I feel it's my bounden duty, before you go farther, to ask your assurances that there'll be no hurt to the lieges, or— what's just as important—to Town property.

MICHAEL : [*Seeing the point*] Now, that's not easy.

FALSE SCOTT : A wouldn't promise.

MICHAEL : Unless, maybe, we weighed them ? Would that suit you ?

FALSE SCOTT : A've no objection. A've stood in the scales before

And up till now it's not been me found wanting.

MICHAEL : Friend Provost, could we have up the Burgh scales ?

PROVOST : Ay, surely, surely. Bellman, bring up the scales !
[*Behind his hand in stage whisper*]
And see that you take the bias off them !

BELLMAN : Ay, ay, Provost ! [*pushing two Dubbities before
him*] Go on, you two ! Fetch up the big town scales !
[*The Bellman and his helpers exit and return shortly with a
huge pair of scales*]

BELLMAN : Set them down there [*front centre*] There !
There !
Will that be all right, sirs ?

MICHAEL : Ay, that seems fine. [*To F. S.*] I hope you're
satisfied ?

FALSE SCOTT : A think so. But there's a small point troubles
me,
If we go in the scales we must leave the pentagons ?

MICHAEL : Well, what about it ? Since we both must
leave them
The risk is equal. We're both equally vulnerable.

FALSE SCOTT : Perhaps. Perhaps. Oh well—oh ! very
well.
[*The two warlocks step out of their pentagons. The False Scott
climbs into one of the pans of the scales and stands there holding
on to the chains. When Michael gets into the other pan it
immediately tips his way*]

MICHAEL : Ha ! Seems you're outweighed already for all
your talk !

FALSE SCOTT : [*Stiffly*] A'm not amused. A assume that
we stairt even ?

MICHAEL : Aye man, you might take a joke ! Ho ! Provost !
Bellman !
Give him his books in with him to tip the balance.

BELLMAN: [*Handing in False Michael's bag of books*] Here
    you are, sir.

[*The scales stay down on Michael's side*]

MICHAEL: What? Are you still down under? Mister
    Provost!

Throw in your chain, and Bellman, you, your baton!

PROVOST: Well, if you say it! but it's most irregular.
    [*He takes off his chain of office and drops it into the scale on
    the False Scott's side. Nothing happens*] Go on now, Bell-
    man. Put your baton in.

[*The Bellman throws in his baton and this time the scales turn
in the False Scott's favour*]

BELLMAN: He! He! That shows the weight that's in
    authority!

MICHAEL: Aye, so I see. Ho, Lazarus!

LAZARUS: Master?

MICHAEL: I see a wild rose lying in the dust there.

It was dropped by Summer when she passed but now.

Let's have it up, lad, to redress the balance.

LAZARUS [*Handing him flower*] Here you are, sir.

MICHAEL: Thank you, lad.

[*As soon as he takes the flower the scales tip sharply in his
favour*].

MICHAEL: What! Are we down again? I'll pluck one
    petal. . . .

[*He does so and throws it away*]

No? Then let's try the next.

[*He throws away another*] Still no? Why then

I'll keep one petal and throw out the flower . . .

[*He does so and this time the scales come even*]

PROVOST: All even now!

MICHAEL: Aye! Aye! Take note my friends! [*Holds up rose petal*] This one light petal of a hedgerow flower
Balances the weight of the civil authority—
Provost and Bellman, Council and strong town jail!
Are you ready, friend?

FALSE SCOTT: A have been ready for quate a long time and if you esk me all this talk is merely an attempt to delay the cursing.

MICHAEL: [*With smile*] Maybe you're right. It was never my forte cursing.
Still, let's get started. I'm set now. Off you go!

FALSE SCOTT: A shall stairt with a comparatively mild one.
[*As he curses the darkness thickens and at the climax there is a thunderclap and lightning flash*]

    Valeat numen triplex Demagorgon!

    Ignei, Aerie, aquitani spiritus!

    Sint mihi dii, Acherontie propitii.

    Surgum Mephistophelis, Dagon quad terminus!

[*Thunder and lightning. The scales turn in the False Scott's favour*]

MICHAEL: Man, but you're old-fashioned, aren't you?
I think I can raise you on that at least!
[*Michael raises his wand*]
[*Pause*]

MICHAEL: Sulphur, saltpeter, charcoal and a lump of lead
An iron tube and a frightened man at the end of it!
[*Again the scales turn with a clang in Michael's favour*]
That knocked your Latin, eh?

FALSE SCOTT: A protest! Gunpowder and firearms are hardly in use yet!

MICHAEL: That's true enough, but then folks like you and

I must take the long view of history. Besides if I was
to go right out of these times altogether—and if I knew
the recipe—I could give you a curse that would make
gunpowder seem as innocent as thorn pollen. Now,
carry on—and if I was you I'd stick to plain Scots this
time.

FALSE SCOTT: [*With sniff*] Kaindly allow me to choose ma
own weapons. If you want to know it's only poor
country wizards that curse in the vernacular now.
[*He tenses himself for a mighty effort. As he does so it grows
darker and darker still, when the storm bursts the darkness
is almost total*]

Ad Acheront! Ad Astorath! Ad Asmodi!

Hel Heloym Sother Emmanuel Sabaoth!

Agra Tellagrammaton Agryos Otheos

Ishyros Athatos Joehova Va Adonei

Saday Homousien Nessias Escherenheys

In manus Luciferus restus perpetuum!

[*This time the thunder rolls long and loud and there are flashes
of sheet lightning following so close on each other that they are
almost continuous. By their light the scales are seen to turn
but this time when they die away the square remains in semi-
darkness*]

MICHAEL: Well, well, well, well, well!

So you're at it again, are you?

Well, let's see if I can give you an answer to that one—

And for all you say I'll stick to my country speech!

Now let's see. Oh! aye. I have it, I think!

But first let's have a light on the subject.

[*Snaps his fingers*] Lights, friends!

[*A soft golden glow illumines the square*]

That's better ! And now for the curse . . .

[*Raises his wand. A pause*]

May you live with relations in a furnished room
In a back street tenement with a lightless stair
With a parcel of quarrelsome bairns and a querulous wife,
With a practising piper above and a cobbler below
And may the chimney smoke !

[*This time the scales go down with such a clatter that the False
Scott is literally thrown out and only saves himself from a fall
by hanging on to the chains. Scrambling up he makes a pass
with his wand at Michael—the end of his wand glowing red
as he does so*]

FALSE SCOTT : Curse you ! Take that !

[*There is a whizzing tearing sound and the true Michael staggers
a little*]

MICHAEL : Oh ! So you're getting personal, are you ?
All right ! I'll meet you there too, and mind ! you
started it.

[*He gets out of the scale and leaps into the relative safety of his
pentagon while the False Scott gets back into his. The light
in the square has faded again and in the dimness we see the
wands of the wizards flash each time they curse. Michael's light
is green and his curses burst about the False Scott in green and
amber bursts. The False Scott's light is red and his curses
explode round Michael in crimson. The Dubbities hide where they
can ; Lazarus crouching behind Michael*]

MICHAEL : Omnia vincit amor, nos et cedamus amori !

[*A burst of green lights*]

FALSE SCOTT : Omnis amaus amens. Odi profanum vulgus
et arceo !

[*A burst of red*]

37

MICHAEL : Cucullus non facit monachum ! Lateat scintillula
forsani.

[*A burst of green*]

FALSE SCOTT : Credat Judæus Apella ! Magna est vis
consultudinis !

[*A burst of red*]

MICHAEL : Magna est veritas et prevalet ! Spes sibi
quisque !

[*A dazzle of green. The False Scott is knocked flat*]

FALSE SCOTT : [*Feebly*] O quam cito transit gloria mundi.
Surgit amari aliquid. Non sum qualis erum !

[*His wand flickers and goes out*]

MICHAEL : [*Triumphantly*] Gaudeamus Igitur ! Sic semper
tyrannis !

[*A golden light now prevails over the scene. Michael throws up
both his arms to heaven*]

By Mars and Mercury ! The apparitions !—I clean forgot
them. Animal !

[*At the word the bear breaks loose and runs to Michael's side
where it crouches down like a dog about to leap*]

MICHAEL : Vegetable !

[*At the word the heap of vegetables on the stall comes to life
as a green man, who, amid the cries of the Dubbities, leaps
down and crouches at Michael's other side. Michael points to
the False Scott, like a huntsman setting on his hounds*]

Fetch him !

[*The bear and the vegetable man rush at the False Scott and
hunt him round the square*]

FALSE SCOTT : Keep them off ! Don't let them near me !
Help !

I give in ! I confess ! Keep them off !

[*The bear and the Vegetable man corner him with his back to the statue, against which he backs gibbering*]

Provost! Bellman! Save me! Call them off!

[*Behind the False Scott the statue slowly straightens itself*]

LAZARUS: Look! The stone man!

TOWNSFOLK: Ooooooh!

MICHAEL: Get him, now!

[*While the bear and the vegetable man close in, the statue grabs the False Scott round the throat from behind, at the same time knocking his hat off, whereupon long grey hair falls about ' his ' shoulders*]

PROVOST: Jumping Josephus! He's not a warlock at all!

LAZARUS: He's not even a man.

VEG. WOMAN: It's Black Minnie the witch!

[*While Michael's familiars struggle with the witch the Dubbities boo her*]

MICHAEL: Away with her! Put her in the pond!

TOWNSFOLK: Aye! Into the pond with her! Booo!

[*The familiars rush Black Minnie, still screeching for mercy, off to the left*]

MICHAEL: [*Raising his hand*] Hush!

[*In the ensuing silence we hear the witch protesting*]

FALSE SCOTT: No! Don't do it! Stop! Stop!

[*Her cries end in a loud splash and a hissing noise as of a hot iron plunged into water, and after a short pause the familiars return. They walk in dead silence up to Michael, bow to him in turn and in turn go back to their places, the statue back on its pedestal, the vegetables back on the stall, the bear to the side of the bear-leader to whom it politely hands back the end of its chain*]

MICHAEL: [*Dusting his hands*] Well, that seems to be that.
I trust Mr. Provost you're in no doubt now
Which is the real Scott and which the faker!
[*During above lighting returns to normal*]

PROVOST: No doubt at all, Your Wizardship! No doubt
at all! But indeed I was sure from the first you were
the right one. And you'll cure Jeannie, sir?

MICHAEL: [*Puzzled*] Jeannie? Who's Jeannie?

PROVOST: My daughter, sir. Her that the fight was
about.

MICHAEL: Was it? Ah yes! I remember now! Dear me!
I had quite forgotten about Jeannie. She's bespelled, I
believe?

PROVOST: That's right, Your Warlockry—and I wouldn't
be surprised but it was that false warlock Black Minnie
that put the spell on her. You'll take it off, Mister Scott?
If you would I'd be much obliged to you.

MICHAEL: Well, I suppose I might as well have a look at
the lass while I'm here. Where is she now?

PROVOST: In the house there, sir. Clear the way, Bellman!
This way, Your Wizardship!

BELLMAN: Out the road there! Clear the way for his most
prussient Warlockry, Mister Michael Scott!
[*Michael slings his mirror over one shoulder and is taking his
bag which Lazarus is still holding when Lazarus speaks*]

LAZARUS: Your Wizardship!

MICHAEL: Aye?

LAZARUS: What about me, Your Wizardship?

MICHAEL: [*Perplexed*] Well, what about you?

LAZARUS: Could you not take me on, sir?

MICHAEL: You want a job with me?

LAZARUS: Oh please, Your Warlockry. I'll serve you faithfully, sir.

I'll carry your books! I'll do whatever you tell me, sir.

[*He clutches the bag of books to him*]

MICHAEL: [*Somewhat embarrassed*] Dear me! What have I done to deserve this?

Why do you want to take service with me, lad?

My fortune leads me by strange roads I warn you!

LAZARUS: What do I care where it leads me so long as I'm with you! Wherever you are must be wonderful, sir!

MICHAEL: [*After staring at him for a moment*]

Man Lazarus, you're not so green as you're cabbage-looking!

All right! You're engaged! Fetch on the luggage!

[*Hands him mirror*]

Lead on to Jeannie, Provost!

PROVOST: This way, Your Worship's Honour! This way, Your Wizardship!

[*While the Dubbities cheer, the Provost bows Michael, followed by Lazarus, into the Provost's house. The door closes behind them and the Dubbities are about to resume their normal activities when there is a stir*]

TOWNSFOLK: What is it?... What's happening?

[*It is the bear. Dragging the bear-leader with it it pushes into the centre of the square where it sits down and lifting up its head gives voice*]

THE BEAR: Cock-a-doodle-doo!

ACT II

A room in the Provost's house. There is a door right and a window left. Michael's magic mirror has been set up close to the wall, with the black cover which is attached to the frame at top and sides, drawn back and pinned by glittering stars to the wall behind. On the window side of the room is a table on which are set out a skull, an hour glass, curiously shaped glasses filled with coloured liquids and a flask which is now bubbling over a spirit lamp. There are two or three big black and brown books on the table and others on the chairs and the floor. On the right side of the mirror are a divan, and, above it, on the wall, a sword. When the curtain rises Michael is discovered at the table, drawing up Jeannie's horoscope. Lazarus is taking out books from the bag and looking at them with much curiosity.

LAZARUS : [*Holding up book*] What's in this one, Mister Scott ?

MICHAEL : [*Without looking up*] What does it say on it ?

LAZARUS : It doesn't say anything on the outside.

MICHAEL : Then try the inside.

[*Lazarus opens the book and turns a page. He turns another. He turns several pages quickly then looks up, extremely perplexed*]

LAZARUS : There's nothing inside either : [*Turns pages rapidly to end of book*] Blank, blank, blank, blank, blank ! There's not a word in it !

42

MICHAEL: Oh, that's my dogmas.

LAZARUS: But I tell you there's nothing in it!

MICHAEL: That's right. I've no dogmas. [*Studies the horoscope*]

[*Lazarus stares, shakes his head, then picks up another book and reads the title*]

LAZARUS: [*To self*] Spells, incantations and curses—Useful on divers occasions. Use with care! [*To Michael*] Mister?

[*Michael does not hear and Lazarus somewhat guiltily opens the book and stares incredulously at the first page. Then he tries another. This is even worse. He reads over words to himself then shakes his head in bewilderment*]

Mister Scott?

MICHAEL: [*Wearily*] Now, what is it?

LAZARUS: [*Bringing book over*] It's this book, sir. It says on the outside, ' Spells, Incantations and Curses—Useful on Divers occasions.' But there's nothing in it but words!

MICHAEL: Well, what do you think spells and incantations are made of, if not words?

LAZARUS: Aye, but these are just words by theirselves! Listen to this: [*Reads*]

Bumfy . . . white . . . black . . . fish . . . trout . . .

Heazle . . . dyke . . . O . . . mithery you're the . . .

Over . . . leery . . . eeerie . . . king . . .

Peenty . . . zeenty . . . jumping . . . heathery

Dyke Jerusalem . . . Dover . . . out!

What does that mean?

MICHAEL: It means whatever you can make it mean.

LAZARUS: How can you make the like of that mean anything?

MICHAEL: How do you make any words mean anything?
By putting them into some sort of order!
You didn't think I used ready-made spells, did you?

LAZARUS: Maybe not, but I still don't get this.
How can you make anything out of this nonsense?
[*Reads*]
Bumfy . . . white . . . black . . . fish . . . trout . . .
Heazle . . . dyke O——

MICHAEL: [*Interrupting*] Ach! Lazarus, you're not wise.
There's other ways of reading than straight forward.

LAZARUS: I thought straight forward was the right way to
read? That's what the teacher said.

MICHAEL: The teacher! The teacher! To the de'il with
the teacher! All the teacher knows is what the other
teacher told him! The right way to read straight forward
—I never heard such nonsense! Man, Lazarus! Don't
you know that some of the most glorious literature in
the world was written backside foremost?

LAZARUS: Was it?

MICHAEL: Aye, was it! And I'm not speaking about the
witches' curse either! How do you think the Book of
Ecclesiastes was written? Backside foremost—every line
of it! How do you think the prophet Isaiah wrote (if he
did write which isn't quite certain)?—Backside foremost!
How do you think Confucius and Lao-Tsze wrote?

LAZARUS: Backside foremost?

MICHAEL: No! See how you fall into habits? Up and
down! Up and down! And they're grand reading
whatever way you take them! No, no, my laddie. Don't
you listen to the teachers. What matters in a book is the
words. The order—that's just the author's prejudice.

LAZARUS : Well, maybe you're right, sir. All the same I
  don't see what you could make out of this lot, however
  you shunted them [*Reads*].
  Bumfy . . . white . . . trout . . . black . . . beazle . . .
  Leery . . . over . . . eerie—No ! it's still nonsense !
MICHAEL : [*With sigh*] Let's have it. [*Takes book*]
  Umph ! You couldn't make much of them it's true.
  Still, you might charm a bairn maybe.
  [*Reciting*]
  Zeenty peenty heathery mithery
  [*Laughs to himself*] Aye ! Maybe it's not original but it's
  fair enchanting !
  [*Jigging as he reads quickly*]
  Zeenty, peenty, heathery mithery
  Bumfy leerie over Dover
  Saw the King of Heazle Peazle
  Jumping over Jerusalem dyke !
  Black fish, white trout !
  Eerie oorie you're out !
  [*On last word he thrusts book into Lazarus's hands*]
  Here, take it !
  Have you fixed the mirror ?
LAZARUS : Aye, but I'm not sure if it's right.
MICHAEL : [*Going to it*] It'll do. It'll do. I don't expect
  that we'll need it but it's as well to have it ready.
LAZARUS : What's it for if it's not asking ?
MICHAEL : If it's not answering, Willie lives in it.
LAZARUS : Who's Willie ?
MICHAEL : A de'il I know. Oh ! you needn't jump ! He's
  a harmless soul so long as you don't try to go through
  the glass. He'd nip the tripes out of anybody that tried

that. But he never comes out of the glass. Would you like to see him ?

LAZARUS : Are you sure it's safe ?

MICHAEL : Oh, it's safe enough. [*Addresses mirror commandingly*] Hi ! Willie, I want you ! [*The mirror slowly lights up and Willie, a fearsome devil with horns and armed and armoured after the Roman fashion, is revealed in it. He salutes Michael and waits at attention*]

MICHAEL : He's waiting for orders.

LAZARUS : What does he do ?

MICHAEL : Brings me things—and anybody I want to have a look at.

LAZARUS : He brings you folk as well as things ?

MICHAEL : Aye, surely. He's never failed me yet, Willie. Mark you ! *They* don't know they've been brought— that's the comic bit of it. But wait, I'll show you. Who would like him to fetch us ?

LAZARUS : Well, since he's a devil let's send him after one of his own kidney. Tell him to fetch in the Bailie-Bellman.

MICHAEL : Whatever you say, lad ! [*To Willie*] Willie ! Fetch us the Bailie-Bellman.

[*Willie salutes, the light fades in mirror. Willie vanishes*]

He won't be long. He's a hellish fast worker, Willie. Ah ! Here he comes.

[*The mirror lights up again. Willie appears again*]

WILLIE : Coming up ! [*He vanishes*]

[*Out of the mirror strolls the semblance of the Bailie-Bellman —as if he was walking down one of the Dubbity streets. He is singing his thoughts to himself as he walks*]

46

BELLMAN : [*Sings*]
> Oh, it's fine to be a Bailie
> To be seated up alof',
> The observed of all observers
> As you tell the bodies off !
> To smile at their excuses
> As they tremble at the rail
> And pack them off by cartloads
> To the old Town Jail !

> Oh la-la la la la-la la-la—lah !
> La la-la-la-la la-la La-lah !
> La la-la la-la la-lah !
> La la-la la-la la-lah !
> Lah la-la la-la la-la la-la la-lah !
> [*He lifts his hat to an invisible passer-by*]
> [*Spoken*]   Good day, Mistress Broon !

[*He is now heading for the mirror*]

BELLMAN : Out of the way there, folks ! Make way for
the Bailie-Bellman ! Don't hold up the town's business !
[*Waving imaginary townsfolk out of the way he exits through
the mirror which immediately blacks out*]

LAZARUS : But that's wonderful, mister ! Can he bring
anybody in like that ?

MICHAEL : Aye, he's a clever devil, Willie.

LAZARUS : [*Indicating mirror*] What sort of place is it back
there ? Where does Willie go when he's not working
for you ?

MICHAEL : Oh Willie goes back to hell.

LAZARUS : You mean hell's through there ?

MICHAEL : Surely. And heaven too of course !

LAZARUS : I thought heaven was up and hell down ?

47

MICHAEL: Who told you that? The schoolteacher again?

LAZARUS: No, it was the priest this time.

MICHAEL: The Sunday School teacher! Don't you listen to him. Up and down are just words, Lazarus. Heaven and Hell are both bits of the same world.

LAZARUS: [*After pause*] No. I don't get it. It seems to me that they're clean contrary to each other.

MICHAEL: What's that to do with it? We all live in the one world here, don't we?

LAZARUS: Aye, I suppose so.

MICHAEL: And some folk have a heavenly existence while for others life's just plain damnable?

LAZARUS: That's true too when you think of it. And it's just the same through there?

MICHAEL: Aye, except that through there you *choose* your company, and that makes an infinite difference. But that's enough of your metaphysics! Do you know anything about horoscopes?

LAZARUS: I'm not sure. I've never seen one before. [*Coming to table*] Is that one?

MICHAEL: [*Studying it*] Aye, Jeannie's and the queer thing about it, Lazarus, is that so far as I can see there's nothing wrong with the lassie.

LAZARUS: Well, maybe there isn't anything wrong with her?

MICHAEL: You know, Lazarus, you'll go a long way in this world or some other one. Even I didn't think of that. [*He crushes up horoscope and tosses it away*] I think we'd better have a look at this lass. Ring the bell, lad.

LAZARUS: Aye, sir.

[*Lazarus pulls a bell-rope and we hear the bell ring in another part of the house. A moment later Provost Peebles, the Laird of Clartydykes and the Bellman appear*]

PROVOST: Are you ready, Your Warlockry? In you go, Laird! In you go, Bellman. Will we bring Jean in, sir?

MICHAEL: Aye, bring her in, Provost. Let's have a look at her.

PROVOST: [*Calling through the house*] Lizzie, fetch Jeannie up! [*To Michael*] This is the Laird of Clartydykes, Your Warlockry. Him Jeannie was to marry when she went off in the dream.

MICHAEL: [*Looking Laird up and down*] I'm not surprised.

LAIRD: [*Seriously*] It was the honour did it, Mister Scott. It's no small matter to have the chance of being mistress of Clartydykes. Oh, but here comes the poor lass now. [*Tugged and pushed by the Provost's wife, Jeannie is manœuvred into the room. There is apparently no volition left in her. Her eyes stare straight before her, wide and expressionless. She moves and stops only as Lizzie moves and halts her*]

PROVOST'S WIFE: Come on! Come on! Hurry up! Don't keep folk waiting. There she is, the besom!

MICHAEL: [*Having looked her up and down*] Put her up on the bed, mistress.

PROVOST'S WIFE: Go on! Get up on the bed! Get up, I said.

[*She gets Jeannie on to the bed where she lies resting on a heap of cushions*]

LAIRD: Don't you think it was the thought of the honour did it?

MICHAEL: There's nothing impossible, Laird. Not even that! But stand clear everybody till I examine her.

49   D

[*Michael takes Jeannie's wrist in his as if feeling her pulse then raises her arm high, and lets it go. The arm falls back limply on the cover. He raises her leg by the ankle in the same way and it too falls limply back*]

Hmm!

[*Bending over her he stares sharply into her face, then, suddenly blows in it, but seemingly there is no reaction. He turns to the Provost*]

MICHAEL: I think that you'd better, Provost, tell me
    exactly how this fit began.

PROVOST: It was either on the morning of the wedding
    Or during the night before. When Lizzie here
    Went up to see was she dolled up for the ceremony
    She found her stretched like this upon the bed
    With no more life in her than a feather bolster!

PROVOST'S WIFE: That's right, Your Warlockry.

LAIRD: It's my opinion, Jeannie just couldn't believe
    I'd really marry her till the glad day came
    And when she realised her glorious fortune
    She was so joyous that she couldn't bear it
    And dropped like that! [*Snaps his fingers*]

MICHAEL: She never showed
    Like signs of queerness in her younger days?

PROVOST: No, no. No more than's usual with a lass!
    It's true she never rightly appreciated
    The signal honour of being the Provost's daughter,
    But then, they're all like that, the young folk now—
    No respect for their elders! No respect
    For anything that is respectable!

PROVOST'S WIFE: I don't agree!

PROVOST: What's that you said?

PROVOST'S WIFE : I said that I don't agree. It's my opinion
   Jeannie's been soft in the head for the best of a year !
   Roaming the hills in her Sunday gown on Mondays !
   Spoiling her best calf shoes in wading mires,
   Idling with ragged shepherds in the twilight,
   Is that wise conduct ?

LAIRD : [*Suspiciously*] What's this ? What's this ?

PROVOST'S WIFE : Reading in books of rhyme !
   Is that wise conduct ? Wanting to marry a shepherd ?
   Is that wise conduct ? No, no, I'll not ' wheest,' Provost.
   The Warlock asked has Jeannie been acting queer.
   I say she has ! But maybe I shouldn't speak
   She's not my bairn.

[*During the above the Provost makes several unsuccessful
attemps to silence his wife and the Laird grows increasingly
agitated*]

LAIRD : [*Suspiciously*] What's this that I'm hearing now
   about a shepherd ?
   Am I to take it the lassie's not heart free ?

PROVOST : Now, now, friend Laird ! Don't get so agitated !
   There's nothing in it. The thing was never serious.
   This herd lad Lizzie speaks of—well, he's glaikit.

PROVOST'S WIFE : [*Throwing in*] Aye, and so's she !

PROVOST : Liz, will you hold your tongue ! He's clean
   daft, Laird,
   As mazed and maddened as a March-month hare.
   Jeannie just liked to tease him—lead him on—
   Oh ! but you know what all these lasslings are !

LAIRD : You're certain sure the thing was never serious ?

PROVOST : [*Solemnly*] Upon my honour, Laird, I swear it's
   true.

When she was serious she thought of you.

LAIRD: [*Joyfully*] She thought of me!

PROVOST: Ever when she was serious.

PROVOST'S WIFE: But when was she ever serious?

PROVOST: Lizzie!
  Now, that's just enough from you! Not another word!
  [*To Michael*]
  I'm sorry, Mister Scott. Forget all that.
  The wife here talks, as usual, out of her turn.
  Jeannie, you take my word, was just lass-usual
  Until she went off in this puzzling dream.

MICHAEL: The good-wife here said that Jeannie was not
    her bairn,
  What does that mean?

PROVOST'S WIFE: It means just what it says. Yon senseless
    zany!
  Yon giddy gosling with her wiles and wimsies,
  You think she's mine? She's no blood kin to me!
  We've got no dafties in my father's family!

MICHAEL: [*To Provost*] Then she's your side?

PROVOST: [*Scratching his head*] Well no, no just exactly.
  Jeannie's a relic of the *ancient* Provost
  Whose widow—when he was called away—poor soul!
  I married. Then, when she went where we all must go
  I married the goodwife here. And so you see
  The lassie there's just daughter by adoption
  [*He claps hands and raises eyes to heaven*]
  Brought up for Christian love and piety.

MICHAEL: [*After pause*] I see!
  [*He has another look at Jeannie*]
  I see! Well, well, my friends, I'll not deceive you.

This matter is more grave than I first thought.
Before I make pronouncement on the case
I must have time to look more fully into it;
Complete her horoscope and take a look
At her basic turba and the centrum naturae.
That's all. Now leave us!
[*Michael goes to table and turns his back on them*]

PROVOST: [*Not pleased*] We're to go out?
[*Michael turns with a large knife, which he begins to sharpen, in his hand*]

MICHAEL: Would you like to stay? For me, there's no
objection.
But when the basic turba's opened up
And when the centrum naturae's fully bare,
I doubt you'll all run risk of being bespelled.
Still, stay if you will—and if you care to risk it!
[*He resumes sharpening of knife*]

LAIRD: [*Nervously*] I think we'd best go out—or me at
least
It's not fair to the lass to take the risk.

PROVOST: Perhaps we'd best all go. Come on now,
Bellman.

BELLMAN: [*Who wants to see operation*] Eh? Oh aye!

PROVOST: Come now, Liz.

BELLMAN: [*Solemnly*] He's going to open up her basic
turba!

LAIRD: [*Solemnly*] And lay the centrum naturae fully bare!

PROVOST'S WIFE: It serves the hussy right!
[*The three exit. The door closes*]

LAZARUS: [*In outburst*] The brock! The toad! The
slithery lying serpent!

The rat ! The eel ! The worm ! the murderous weazel !

MICHAEL : I take it you're referring to the Provost ?

LAZARUS : Who else ? The slinking stoat ! The creeping
    Judas !

Did you hear him, mister ? He brought Jeannie up
Out of the Christian charity of his heart.
Him and his Christian charity ! It's Jeannie here
That brought him to all he is ! He's just the Provost
By right of wardship !

MICHAEL : By right of wardship ? How ?

LAZARUS : Because the right

Comes aye with the lassie-line for certain reasons
Maybe more obvious in Dubbity than elsewhere !
At any rate, whoever weds with Jeannie—
Tinker or tailor, soldier, sailor, thief—
Becomes the Provost. If the lass wed me
I'd be the Provost ! Aye, and if I were
I'd sort Sir Davie, I can tell ye, mister !

MICHAEL : This puts a new complexion on the matter.
Aye, altogether ! [*Going to Jeannie*] If this lass could speak
Just for five minutes, I've an inkling, Lazarus
She'd tell us a queer-like tale. Ho ! Jeannie ! Jeannie !
We're all friends here. Will you not wake a wee ?
[*Blows in her face*]
No ? Still in the dream ? Well, well, there's nothing
    for it,
We must try sterner measures. Lazarus !

LAZARUS : Sir ?

MICHAEL : Turn up the lamp !
[*Lazarus does so*]
Heat up the boiling lead !

We'll try a cup of that poured down her gullet,
And if that fails . . . [*He whispers into Lazarus's ear*]

LAZARUS: [*Horrified*] Angels defend! Oh, poor wee, poor
  wee lassie!
  A red-hot bollus thrust deep in her . . . .
  Will it not hurt, mister?

MICHAEL: Aye, hurt most horrible!
  [*Behind, Jeannie sits up apprehensively*]
  Or would if the lass were conscious—[*He turns quickly
  but Jeannie is down again*]
                              Once, friend Lazarus
  There was a lass just like our Jeannie here
  Who let on for some purpose of her own
  She'd been bespelled. Put on swooning act
  Aye, and maintained it—but I'll say no more
  What's subsequent to that would goose your soul!
  Is the lead near boiling?

LAZARUS: It's just on the point.

MICHAEL: We'll give it a minute yet. It's most important
  It should be right on the boil or else it might
  Clot in the gizzard and stop up her speech.
  And yet it mustn't be too heated either—
  Else it might never reach the major turba
  But burn its way straight out by the nape of her neck.
  Let's see it now. [*Looks into vessel*]
  [*Behind him, Jeannie, giving in, sits up*]

JEANNIE: Mister!

MICHAEL: Dear me! The lassie's awake. Now
  Isn't that wonderful! That just shows you, Lazarus!
  You said my books were only words but look!
  Bare words have worked as well as boiling lead!

55

JEANNIE : Oh Mister Scott, please, please don't tell the
Provost.

MICHAEL : Tell him of what, lass ?

JEANNIE : Tell him I'm not bespelled. I'll never marry
That wizened kale-root of a half-wit laird
Whatever they do to me ! Master, have mercy on me !
I'd rather drink your boiling lead ! I'd rather
Have the burning red hot bollus thrust deep in—
Wherever you meant to put it ! Mister Scott !
Don't you take sides against me. Help me, please !
[*She begins to weep*]

MICHAEL : [*Stroking her hair*] There, there, my lass, there's
no cause here for weeping
Trust to old Michael Scott to see you right !
I'll not beguile you. But if we're to help,
First we must know the cause of all the upset.
Why's Provost Peebles so intent on this wedding ?
Why does he throw this half-wit at your head ?
Here! [*Gives his handkerchief*] Dry your eyes,
Aye ! blow your nose as well !
[*Jeannie does so*]
Tell all you know and then, maybe, we'll see
If there's no way to give this rascal Peebles
What he deserves ! Come now ! Speak up ! Say first
Why does he want to marry you to this Laird ?

JEANNIE : Must I tell that ?

MICHAEL : Aye, must ! I must know all !

JEANNIE : Well, if you must know, he and the Bailie-
Bellman
Have dipped so deep in the Dubbity Town Chest
They've scraped the foot clean-clear of the tint of silver,

And now they're afraid if I wed with an honest man
The tale of their theft will reach the ears of the town.
At least that's half the tale. The other half
Is this : this half-wit laird has promised them
Once we are wed he'll cover up the thieving,
Fill up the chest with gold, and when that's done,
Resign the Provost's honour to Sir Davie
So he and the Bellman can start on the game again !

LAZARUS : Man, but I knew it ! It's the common talk
Of the Dubbity streets. Your Warlockry
It was for saying precisely what Jeannie's said
That I was put in the pillory by the Bellman !

MICHAEL : Was that the way of it, lad ? Ah, well, we'll—
But finish the tale, lass. Go on, finish the tale !

JEANNIE : That's all, Your Wizardship. That's all I know.

MICHAEL : Oh no, my lass. Not half ! Have you forgotten.
Running about the hill braes on a Monday
In your Sunday gown ? Spoiling your fine calf shoes
Wading in mires and dubs ? Have you forgot
A certain herd lad by the name . . . ?

JEANNIE : [*Confused*] O' Jock !

MICHAEL : Oh, so it's Jock ! Well, well, who is the lad
And what's his role in this romantic story ?
What's the lad like ?

JEANNIE : I'm not right sure except that—oh, he's braw !
With such great eyes—they're either brown or blue
I'm not sure which, for when he looks at me
My own swim so. He has a mouth—
O such a mouth ! A queer wee, dear wee mouth !
With a queer wee quirk here where the corner turns ;
And when I look at it, it's like a hand

Gripped on my heart and squeezed and squeezed and
    squeezed . . .
And when he speaks he says such queer-like things!
After they seem just daft, but at the time,
Listening, you lose all heaviness as if
At the next word you'd soar away in the sky,
Light as the down bairns blow from the yellow clockweed
Telling the hour. The folk here say he's daft
Because his head's so wrapped about in the clouds
There's not a slough on the moor he doesn't splash in
But if he's moon-struck, then I'm moon-struck too
For oh I love him! Oh I do! I do!
Would he were here!

MICHAEL: You'd like to see him?

JEANNIE: Aye, but it cannot be.

The Provost would have him flung straight into jail
If he came here.

MICHAEL: De'il take the Provost! We'll bring him in, lass,
By ways that no Provost knows. Here by the glass.
[*He goes to and addresses the magic mirror*]
Hi, Willie! I want you. Now, Jeannie, you mustn't
fear.
This fiend's my servant and he'll never hurt you.
[*The glass lights up and Willie appears*]

MICHAEL: Willie, away up to the high green braes
And fetch us down the lad they call Jock the Herd.
[*Willie salutes and vanishes*]
Now, Jeannie, you mustn't speak when Jock appears
Else you might hurt him.
[*The mirror slowly lights up again and Willie appears*]

WILLIE: Coming up! [*He vanishes*]

[*Now Jock appears in it. He comes out backwards, calling and whistling to his dogs, for to his mind he is still on the hill with his sheep. He whistles shrilly*]

JOCK: [*Addressing dogs*] Come ahint, Sheena! Get in there, Bran. Drewie, you devil! Come ahint, I said! That's it! That's it! [*The invisible dogs are now close and he half turns*] Sit down there and behave yourselves. [*He pushes away one which is jumping up and fawning on him*] Down! Down! Get down man! Man Bran, we'll never make a sheepdog of you if you carry on like that! Down sir! Sit down like Sheena there. That's it. That's better! [*He sees a flower and stoops and plucks it and picks off the petals*] She loves me . . . she loves me not. . . . She loves me . . . She loves me not. . . . She loves me . . . She loves me n—— [*Notices it is the last petal and throws it away irritably*] Ach! The sheep's been at it! [*Picks another*] She loves me . . . She loves me not. . . . She loves me . . . She loves me not. . . . [*Counts remaining petals quickly*] She loves me . . . She loves me not. . . . She loves me . . . She loves me not. [*Pause, then ecstatically*] She loves me! [*Holds up last petal and kisses it, then heaving a deep sigh leans on his crook and gazes dreamily into distance*] Oh, Jeannie lass, if you were only here!

JEANNIE: [*Stepping forward*] But Jock I——

MICHAEL: [*Taking her arm*] Hush, Jeannie. You mustn't speak to him.

JOCK: [*Leaning on his staff*] Here on these hills I tend my sheep
With Sheena, Bran and Drewie.
But in my thoughts it isn't sheep
I'm tending, Jean, but you ay!

Oh Jeannie, Jeannie, if we love
Why cannot we ensue it ?
Oh love, I love you far too well
I fear me I shall rue it !
[*He sighs another deep sigh then half-turns and gazes as if up
the hill, shading his eyes against the sun. Then sharply :*]
Sheena ! Bran ! You too, Drewie ! After them quick !
Get them back off the edge there ! Good lass
Sheena ! That's it, Bran ! Go on, you're doing fine !
We'll make a sheepdog out of you yet, boy.
Down ! Down ! That'll do now. Come ahint now !
[*He faces forward again and heaves another heavy sigh*]
Oh Jeannie ! I wonder if you're feeling as bad as I am ?
JEANNIE : I'm sure I am, Jock.
MICHAEL : Hush !

JOCK : The worst of it is that it's all my own fault. If I
were like one of the lads in the daft old fairytales I
suppose I would just up with my crook, send the sheep
to the devil and go marching down into Dubbity there
and carry her off like a lamb on my shoulder. And mind
you ! If I don't do it, it's not that I'm afraid. . . . At
least, it's not *just* that I'm afraid. It's just that when I
go down there into that great bustling town I feel so
bashful. And then, Jeannie, what can I bring you ?—
except a handful of flowers ? [*Sighing*]
Oh were I rich as Crœsus was
Oh then I'd deck you fair, lass !
With a silken gown and a golden chain
And pearls to hang in your hair, lass !
Were I but rich as yon old Laird
I would not be so backward !

I'd give you [*Impatiently*]—Ach! What can I give?
I haven't got the cash for't!

Get out of there, Sheena!

[*He kicks an imaginary dog out of his way, then as it retreats with an inaudible yelp, he looks contrite*]

Oh! Did I hurt you, Sheena? Come here, lass. Let's see it. [*He kneels and examines the invisible dog's paw*] I'm sorry, Sheena, I didn't mean to be coarse with you. [*He strokes the invisible dog's head fondly*] There, there, you're all right now, aren't you? Bonnie Sheena! Wise Sheena! You don't care what sort of clothes I wear, do you? Or whether I've a penny in my purse or not? Aye, if the world were but folked with Sheenas it would be a better world for shepherds! [*Suddenly he looks up hill, and scrambles hastily to his feet*]

Hell burn the mutton-heads! They're off for that edge again! Come on, lass! Come on, you two, let's up to them. [*Sees another flower and picks it, and exits through the glass with :*] She loves me . . . She loves me not. . . . She loves me . . . She loves me not. . . . She loves me . . . She loves . . .

[*He re-enters the mirror, the light fades, and he is gone*]

MICHAEL : Well, well, well, well, well! So that's Jock, is it?

JEANNIE : He's braw, isn't he?

MICHAEL : Well, so long as you think so I suppose that's all that matters. Och well, no doubt we'll be able to make something of him between us. But the main point is, what are we going to do with the Provost?

LAZARUS : Could you not blast him, mister, like you blasted the bell?

MICHAEL: Aye, doubtless I could. But no! No Lazarus.
There's no finesse about a simple blasting.
I doubt e'en wizardy would lose its charm
If it was used in such a wholesale fashion,
There's surely some more subtle way than that
To trip the heels up of these jinking Johnnies.
If we could somehow make them serve *our* ends
Catch them in their own snares, set them to dig
The very pit-hole into which they stumble . . .

LAZARUS: If we could get them to marry Jean to Jock
That would upset their applecarts just splendid.

MICHAEL: It would. It would! Man, Lazarus, you've
hit it!
Listen now, Jeannie. Here's what we three must do.
[*Michael whispers in Jeannie's ear and Lazarus presses close
to hear. At first Jeannie looks dubious*]

JEANNIE: Are you quite sure, master, that they'll think
of him?

MICHAEL: Aye, sure, dead sure! Don't fear. And after
that . . .
Come close in now. Come close . . .
[*Jeannie and Lazarus come close and Michael goes on whispering.
As he whispers Jeannie begins to smile and nod and Lazarus
the same and, in the end, as the curtain falls, they are both
smiling and nodding like China mandarins*]

ACT III

SCENE ONE

The same room a few minutes later. Lazarus is discovered pulling the bell rope. Jeannie is back on the divan, and Michael standing by the table looking at one of his books. The door opens and the Provost, the Provost's wife, the Laird and the Bellman-Bailie enter.

PROVOST : Are you ready, Your Wizardship ?

MICHAEL : [*Looking up with a start*] What's that ? Oh aye, come in !

LAIRD : Have you examined her, Your Magicianship ? Can you work a cure ?

MICHAEL : That's to be seen. Meanwhile I've consulted oracles,
Worked out the configuration of the stars and planets,
Drawn up her horoscope, and compounded here
[*He lifts high a small vial of green liquid*]
A magic potion which I guarantee
Will make the patient more or less herself—
But for one hour !

PROVOST : [*Perplexed*] An hour ?

PROVOST'S WIFE : [*To Bellman*] An hour !

BELLMAN : [*To Laird*] An hour !

LAIRD : Only an hour ?

MICHAEL : Only an hour. To work a lasting cure
There's stronger magic needed.

63

LAIRD : What exactly's the matter with the lassie ?
  It's not like plague and that ? It's not infectious ?
MICHAEL : Oh, most infectious !
  [*The Laird and group retreat hurriedly*]
MICHAEL : Perilous infectious !
  But let me see. Perhaps I'd best explain
  The whole thing to you ?
BELLMAN : Do !
PROVOST : I wish you would.
MICHAEL : [*Seating himself on the table's edge*]
  Well then, listen, first to my diagnosis.
  You're right enough the lass has been bespelled
  By a most powerful magic—namely Amor !
PROVOST : Amor ?
PROVOST'S WIFE : Amor ?
LAIRD : Amor ?
BELLMAN : Amor ?
MICHAEL : Amor ! Ah well, that's not so bad. I have
  A charm, no doubt, that would have dealt with that
  Had I been called in time. The trouble is
  In the first place the long delay there's been
  Since she was first bespelled, and even more
  The lassie's own condition at the time,
  For, as the goodwife here, will surely know,
  When lasses come to Jeannie's age they live
  Under the influence of the Planet Venus,
  And when that light's conjuncted with the moon's
  The things that happen would astonish you !
  They put up no resistance to this Amor.
  Indeed they welcome it ! They run to meet it !
  With their own hands they thrust the poisoned dart

Into their hearts—and once the heart is touched,
Ah! then it's serious.

PROVOST: [*To wife*] It's serious!

PROVOST'S WIFE: [*To Laird*] Serious!

LAIRD: [*To Bellman*] Serious!

BELLMAN: How serious?

MICHAEL: Near mortal serious! You see that's still
not all.

PROVOST: [*To Wife*] That isn't all!

PROVOST'S WIFE: [*To Laird*] And that's not all!

LAIRD: [*To Bellman*] It isn't all!

BELLMAN: God save us all!

MICHAEL: Not nearly all. In fact it's not the half of it!
Up to that point the case is fairly simple
But from there on the complications grow
As thick as groundsel after summer showers
In well-dunged gardens when folk fare away
This magic I call Amor—Amas Amor!
Has played the devil with her blood and juices!
Her bile's near boiling and her gall and spleen
—In opposition to the rays of Mercury—
Have overflowed and drowned the centrum naturæ,
Causing—as you, Sir Davie, would expect—
A counter-generating in the basic turba,
Which, I need hardly add's given rise in turn
To much resurgum of the morbid fluxes,
Leading in their turn to a quaky fundament,
Collapse of the blastodermus, and all the rest of it!
You follow me?

PROVOST: Eh? Oh ay, more or less, more or less. Carry
on, sir!

MICHAEL: Well, so far it's not so difficult, but from there on
　　The thing's more subtle.　　You must understand,
　　If you're to make sense of this poor maid's condition,
　　There are two principles in the centrum magnum
　　Each with its growth, decay, and that a third,
　　Still without name, but lodged down beneath the sweet-
　　　　breads—
　　And governed mainly by the sphere of Jupiter—
　　Keeps the first two in check, preserves the ternary,
　　Conserves the balance in the omni-genetrix—
BELLMAN: [*dazedly*] The omni-genetrix?
MICHAEL: The omni-genetrix and the nicromantia,
　　Which in their turn act on the centrum naturæ,
　　Allay the craving in the major magnia,
　　Soothe down the magus and preserve the unity.
　　But that's in health! Whereas in Jeannie's case—
PROVOST: The magnia's craving?
MICHAEL: Precisely, Provost.　Most concisely put!
PROVOST'S WIFE: And is there nothing that can put her
　　　　right?
　　Restore the balance in the centrum naturæ?
LAIRD: Sooth down these magus?
BELLMAN: Unite the unities?
MICHAEL: There is one way the balance might be restored
　　But oh! my friends there is such danger in it
　　I'm loath to name it.
PROVOST: Hoots! Hoots! Speak up! Tell us what this
　　　　cure is.
　　Whatever the peril is the lass must bear it.
　　It's for my good—*her* good!—What is the remedy?
MICHAEL: [*Solemnly*] Marriage.

66

PROVOST : [*Incredulously*] Marriage ?
PROVOST'S WIFE : [*The same*] Marriage ?
LAIRD : [*The same*] Marriage ?
BELLMAN : [*The same*] Marriage ?
PROVOST : B-but how can the lassie wed froze up like that ?
MICHAEL : Oh, that's soon mended. As I said before
   By virtue of the magic in this potion
   Which is compounded of a unicorn horn,
   Yolk of a harpie's egg, the sifted dust
   Out of the coffin of an Egyptian king ;
   The whole well-shaken with plain Eden water
   On a Black Friday when the moon was blue ;
   Jeannie will wake and be herself one hour,
   During which time if she is firmly wed
   Her cure is certain.
PROVOST : Man, but that's wonderful !
PROVOST'S WIFE : It's just ideal !
LAIRD : Aye, Sir, it's marvellous !
BELLMAN : If not miraculous !
PROVOST : [*Bustling forward*]
   We'll do it now. Give her the magic potion.
   Here's the good Laird just burning to be wedded !
LAIRD : Aye, aye, as soon's you like !
BELLMAN : I'll cry the priest !
PROVOST : Aye, cry him quick. We've lost enough of time !
MICHAEL : Hold on ! Don't be so fast. You've not heard
      all yet !
PROVOST : Hoots ! Hoots ! We've heard enough—
MICHAEL : You've not heard half yet !
   Whoever's to marry Jeannie should first know
   The whole extent and scope of the consequences !

Hearken now, Laird! Whoever marries Jeannie
While she's infected with this catching Amor,
As sure as my name's Michael that man'll get it
Within a twelvemonth he'll be as Jeannie's now!
[*A pause*]
LAIRD: Sir, is this true?
MICHAEL: As true as death!
PROVOST: [*Recovering*]

Oh come on, Laird! What's all the hesitation?
You'll have a year; at your age that's a life!
LAIRD: No, no, not me. I'm not as daft as that!

To be as she is in a year? Oh! no!
It's true that I'm sorely smitten with the lass,
But to be set fast like a calf's foot jelly!
Stilled like a snowman in fine skating weather!
No! no! Not me! Man, think what she might be up to
When the Amor struck me!—under my very nose
Flirting with gallants at my own hall table!
Showing them round the house; in my bedchamber—
Oh! I can hear her now: " Aye, that's the Laird.
No, no, he can't see us—or if he sees
What in the world can the poor man do about it?"
To the De'il with even the thought of such a torment!
Whoever marries her it'll not be me!
Let the shepherd have her!
PROVOST: Now there's a thought!

Tell me, Your Wizardship, supposing now—
Oh! just for argument's sake, you know—
Some other man than the Laird here married Jeannie,
And that man well—well, let's say that he died.
Would the cure still hold?

MICHAEL: Of course! Why not? Once Jeannie's wed
she's cured.

PROVOST: [*Rubbing his hands*] She is? Man, man, that's fine.
Now suppose again—
Still for the sake of argument!—that after
Jeannie was wed again, the next to marry her
Would have no need to fear this plaguey Amor?
He'd never freeze up?

MICHAEL: No. Not him.
But what's the import of these many questions?

PROVOST: Just this, I'm almost sure that I know a suitor
Who's such a nit-wit—I mean such a hero!
He'd cut his gullet with a joiner's saw
To pleasure Jeannie!

PROVOST'S WIFE: Is it Jock the Herd that you mean—
yon foolish rhymer?

PROVOST: Hush! Lizzie. Hush! That's most uncharitable.
Were Jock not foolish he would never serve us!
Bellman away—

PROVOST'S WIFE: But what's the good—

PROVOST: I'll tell you the good, good wife, when we're
alone!
Now Bellman away, cry Jock, and cry the priest.
[*In stage whisper and with meaningful wink*]
And cry the Town Guard too!

BELLMAN: Eh? Oh aye! I see.
[*He winks back and exits*]

PROVOST: Your Wizardry?

MICHAEL: Well, Provost?

PROVOST: At times like these a father's heart's so full
With thoughts of grace and Providence and the like

He needs a bit of privacy, a space
For meditation thanks-giving and prayer.
Come Lizzie [*Takes her arm*]

PROVOST'S WIFE : But——

PROVOST : Now hold your tongue ! Come, Laird !
[*Takes Laird's arm and the three exit—Jeannie sits up looking distressed*]

JEANNIE : Oh, Mister Scott, did you hear what the Provost said ?
When Sir Davie speaks of Providence and grace
It's certain evidence he's planning evil !

MICHAEL : Well, we'll soon see. We'll bring him in,
Here by the glass and see what the rascal's up to.
[*He goes over to the mirror*]
Hi ! Willie. I want you !
[*The mirror lights up and Willie appears*]
Fetch us the Provost !
[*Willie bows and vanishes*]
Now, mind ! not a word from either of you !
[*The mirror lights up slowly and Willie appears*]

WILLIE : Coming up ! [*He vanishes*]
[*The Laird appears in the glass. Beckoning to the Provost and Lizzie (who are invisible) he backs out into the room*]

PROVOST : Shut the door, Laird. Aye ! Lock it, lock it.
Come over here and gather about me close !
[*To the invisible Lizzie*]
And you, stop your bubbling, Liz. It doesn't help us.
Besides there's no need to wail. I have a plan
And man ! a fine one, to clear up this tangle !
Laird, are you sure that door's right locked ? You are ?

Well well, that's fine. Losh ! But the window's wide !
[*He goes through motions of closing the window*]
Wait till I close it. There ! We're all safe now
From chance eavesdroppers. It would hardly do
If what I've to tell to you two in here
Were heard in the public street. The Dubbities
Are maybe a wee thing backward in the uptake
But were they to hear their Provost—what's that, Laird ?
Come to the point ? Man, I must say it's evident
You've no acquaintance with what's called procedure !
But I'm the Provost and I will observe
All due formalities though we're plotting murder !
JEANNIE : [*Her hand at her mouth*] Murder !
PROVOST : [*As if answering the Laird*]
Aye, murder ! What's the matter with you, Laird ?
You don't like the sound of the word ? Well then, let's
    say—
Say liquidation of a black obstruction
To the common weal—that's ours of course ! You agree ?
Ah well, that's fine. The amendment is accepted !
Now here is my plan. We'll get this silly warlock—
MICHAEL : Eh ?
[*The Provost pushes away the invisible Lizzie*]
No ! No ! How can he hear ? We'll get this warlock
With his magic potion to wake Jean the hour :
Wed her to Shepherd Jock—Now, Lizzie ! Lizzie !
Just hold your tongue and hear me out to an end !
We'll wed her to Jock I say, then here's the point !
Soon as the job is done, the last aye said,
We'll whip him away and put him down in the dungeon !
Upon what charge ? Upon what charge, did you say ?

Leave it to me, to find the charges for you.
A dozen if you would like! They say the lad
Writes rhymes and ballads—that's red crime enough
To take him up on! But the point is this!
Once we have got him jailed, our friend the Bellman
Will, for a crown or two—that's your part, Laird!
See that shepherd's dinner gets clean forgot
Say for a week—and if that doesn't work . . .
There's other ways . . . ! Ay, Liz? You still don't see
How that will help us? Woman, have you no wits?
When Jeannie's married that damned spell comes off!
When Jock's been mur—dealt with, then she'll be a
    widow!
When she's a widow, then the Laird can marry her!
That's the whole plan. For me I think it's dandy!
It might work, Laird? It will! It just can't fail.
What's that, Liz? Did I hear you saying "immoral?"
Are you accusing the Provost of being immoral?
Well, that's what it sounded like! No, no,
It's not for ourselves. It's all for the public good.
It's not immoral that you're meaning, Lizzie.
The word's 'expedient.' How can I put back
The money borrowed from the Burgh funds
Unless we can get Jean wed to the honest Laird?
Unless the Laird . . . ? No, no. I didn't expect it.
You see, good wife, there's no way out but this.
I'm sorry that Jock must die, but well, that's life!
And in the way we're doing the lad a service.
His life it's plain's not worth a broken button
But by his death he'll serve the town and me!
Well, what do you say? Do you accept the plan?

You do? That's fine! Here. Let's all have a drink
on it!

[Searches on imaginary shelf for bottle]

Where is that bottle? Have you seen it, Lizzie?

In the wee cupboard? Where—Oh, aye! I see!

*[In his search for the bottle the Provost re-enters the mirror.
The light fades and he vanishes. There is a moment of silence
then Lazarus explodes]*

LAZARUS : The old blackguard!

JEANNIE : *[Anxiously]* What'll we do, sir? Can you warn
poor Jock?

Stop him from coming since it's to his death?

MICHAEL : Wheest, lassie, wheest! This needs consideration.

[He thinks]

Jeannie, you're certain sure that you want this shepherd?

JEANNIE : Aye sure, but not, oh! not at such a cost!

MICHAEL : If we go on put all the cost to me, lass.

I'll settle all bills, aye! and pay them with interest!

" That silly warlock "—Losh! I'm quite agitated!

Listen to me now, Jeannie. Here's what we'll do.

We'll let them bring Jock in. We'll have the wedding

And after, well after you must just trust me.

JEANNIE : You'll not let them hurt Jock.

MICHAEL : *[Raising his hand]* By this hand I swear it!

But quick! Lie down. I hear a stir on the stair!

Here they come back.

*[Jeannie lies down as before. There is a knock at the door,
and the Provost, Provost's wife, Laird, Bellman, Jock, Priest
and Town Guard enter. The Town Guard is a tough-looking*

individual armed with a pike. The Priest, who is suffering
from a tremendous cold, carries a book under his arm]

PROVOST : [*Cheerily*] Here we are again ! Go on, Jock.
There's no need to be shy. The lassie's waiting.
[*Jock is in such an ecstasy that he does not even notice Jeannie.*
He looks around him in happy bewilderment]

JOCK : Is this the room where my dear Jeannie lives ?
O happy room ! O would I were this room !
Is this the floor trod by the feet of Jeannie ?
O happy floor ! O would I were this floor !
Is that the chair where my dear Jeannie sits ?
O happy chair ! O would I were that chair !
Is that the bed where my dear Jeannie lies ?
O happy bed ! O would I were—
[*The Provost has a fit of coughing*]

PROVOST : Aye ! aye ! later on, later on !
Meanwhile I think you'll notice if you'll take a look
The lassie's in it. [*To Michael*] He's fair o'ercome !
[*Jock drops on his knees by the side of the couch and timidly*
takes Jeannie's hand]

JOCK : Oh Jeannie, Jeannie, can it be
That you're to marry me, love ?
How comes it that a lass like you
Can love a lad like me, love ?
I worshipped you ay from afar
I never hoped for more, lass.
How could I hope, since I was earth
And you were light and air, lass ?
Oh Jeannie, you are fresh and fair
As mountain flowers in May, lass

74

And me, I'm like a mountain bear—

But oh! I love you true, lass!

[*He gazes at Jeannie yearningly*]

MICHAEL: [*To Provost*] Does he know?

PROVOST: About the consequences? Well, not precisely—

MICHAEL: How much precisely does he know?

PROVOST: Well, precisely nothing as yet. I thought he might

Find it a bit discouraging.

MICHAEL: I'll tell him

It's simple justice that the lad should learn

Just what he's stepping into. Ho, there Jock!

[*Jock rises*]

JOCK: You want me, sir?

MICHAEL: Aye. Hearken now, your future hangs upon it.

There lies your Jeannie. Yonder there stands the priest.

Here in this glass (*lifts it*) I have a magic potion

Which will make Jeannie well enough to wed

But you must know before the vows are made

Who weds with Jeannie pays a price for it!

The words that will work her well may work him woe.

Within a year of the wedding knot's first tying

He that weds her will be as she is now!

JOCK: You said a year?

MICHAEL: A year. No more, no less. Exact a year.

JOCK: [*Giddy with his good fortune*]

O happy year! O happy happy year!

To have my Jeannie for my very own

Twelve months, weeks fifty-two, three six five days—

And it's a leap year so it's three six six!

75

O happy leap year !—eight seven eight four hours
In heaven ! Five two seven o four o minutes—
And every minute with its load of blisses !
Thirty-one, six two two four hundred seconds—
And every second winged away with kisses !
O happy fate ! Ye stars what have I done
That fate should shower on me such blessed fortune ?

MICHAEL : You'll pay the cost then ?

JOCK : There is no cost. It's privilege !
And were the time an hour I'd say the same.
To think as I grow stiff that she'll grow supple !
To know as my blood geals hers will run warm !
Why ! That's my happiness ! I'm no book hero.
But I love Jeannie, and I love her true.

MICHAEL : I believe you do !

PROVOST : [*Briskly*] Aye. Aye. I'm sure we all applaud
the sentiment.
But if the warlock's ready, let's wake Jean up.
The priest here rose up from his bed to serve
And if we keep him standing here too long
I wouldn't wonder if his next engagement
Was playing the leading man at his own funeral !

PRIEST : That's true ! Achoooo !

MICHAEL : So be it then ! Stand back now while I place
A single drop of this most priceless fluid
Fair on her lips. [*He does so*] There now, it's done.
Within six wing-beats of the great grey goose
You'll see her wake.

[*Michael stands back, there is a pause, then Jeannie stirs, sighs,
smiles and sits up*]

JEANNIE : Oh Jock ! Is it you ?

JOCK: [*Throwing himself on his knees and kissing her hand*]
  Aye Jeannie, it's me.

PROVOST: Now, isn't that wonderful?

PROVOST'S WIFE: It's simply marvellous!

LAIRD: It's most astonishing!

BELLMAN: I'd say miraculous!

PRIEST: I'd say—achoooo!

PROVOST: [*Pulling Jock away from Jeannie*]
  Now now, stop that! There isn't the time and place
  For such like ticklings, cuddlings, osculations!
  Rise up my lass! You see the priest over there?

JEANNIE: Oh, am I dying? Is that why I'm so happy?

PROVOST: Dying! No, no. He's come to marry you
  To this lad here.

JEANNIE: To Jock?

PROVOST: Aye, aye, to Jock, now stir yourself and let the
    reverend father—

PRIEST: Achoooo!

PROVOST: Unite you two. And may a father's blessing
  Rest on the ceremony—and on what will follow it!
  [*Jeannie rises*]

JEANNIE: You really mean you'll let me wed with
  Jock?

PROVOST: I do! Get started, Father, and keep it short.
  We'll have the prayers on Sunday. For the now
  Stick to the strict essentials. You have your book?

PRIEST: [*Nodding*] Achoo! Achoooo!

PROVOST: Then let's get on with it!

PROVOST'S WIFE: [*Suddenly*] Oh, I can't stand it!
  [*She bursts into noisy weeping*]

PROVOST: [*Annoyed*] Now, Lizzie! Lizzie!

77

PROVOST'S WIFE: She looks so bonnie! O the poor wee
    lassie!

PROVOST: Liz! Will you wheest! Here! come away over
    here.

[*He leads Lizzie aside*]

Sit down quiet and don't disturb the proceedings.

It's all right, friends. She always cries at a wedding.

Carry on, Father. Bellman, ring out the bell.

[*The Bellman rings his bell*]

Now go on, Father!

PRIEST: [*In a sniffling chant, interrupted by sneezes*]

Jock of the Braes, otherwise known as the shepherd
    laddie [*Sniff*]

Do you take this Achoo! now standing beside you
    [*Sniff*]

To be joined to you in the state of matrimony

Which has been ordained for the avoidance of Achoo!

And other things that there's no need to mention
    [*Sniff*]

Will you [*Sniff*] whatever the provocation try aye to
    love her.

Humour her as much as possible [*Sniff*] see she never
    wants Achooo!

House-room, [*Sniff*] fire-warmth, and enough of Achoo!

Will you promise never to affront her by chasing stranger
    lasses

Or if that's beyond you [*Sniff*] at least keep it quiet from
    her?

If you imagine you can do all that, will you now say
    Achooo!

JOCK: Achoooo!

[*The Bellman rings his bell and there is a general outbreak of coughing and nose-blowing, above which the voice of the Provost's wife, torn with sobs rises*]

PROVOST'S WIFE: O the poor wee lassie! The poor wee lassie!

PROVOST: Wheest, Lizzie! Wheest! We're near half-ways there.

[*The Bellman rings*]

PRIEST: [*Addressing Jeannie now*]

And now you, Jeannie, do you take this laddie [*Sniff*]
To be joined unto you in the state of Achoo!
Will you do whatever he says however nonsensical.
Give him his meat on time [*Sniff*] See his shirts are mended [*Sniff*]
Keep him in work and out of it, forsaking Achooo!
Humour him as much as possible [*Sniff*] never affront him
By throwing your bonnet after stranger laddies
[*Sniff*] Or if that's impossible at least keep it quiet from him.
If you think you can do all that will you now say Achooo!

JEANNIE: Oh, I do!

PRIEST: Put the ring on her finger.

JOCK: I haven't—

MICHAEL: [*Giving his*] Here, take this.

JOCK: Oh, thank you, sir. [*He puts ring on Jeannie's finger*]
Oh, Jeannie!

JEANNIE: Oh, Jock!

PRIEST: And now in the name of Achoo! I pronounce these—
Achoos! before me wedded man and wife
Past all redemption!

[*Shuts book and turns immediately to Provost with his hand out*]
Will you pay me now, sir?

PROVOST: [*Waving him off*] Later on! Later on. Now I've
　got work to do.

[*Magisterially*] Friends, your attention. I've doleful news
　for you.

Even while the priest was tying the sacred knot
Between poor Jeannie and the shepherd lad there
The Bellman has brought me in word this very lad

BELLMAN: [*Surprised*] What's this?

PROVOST: [*Unheeding interruption*]

Has done such crimes against the common weal
Such as I daren't name before the priest,
So black they are! Wherefore, though I am loath
To cast a shadow on this bright occasion
I have no option in my dual capacity
Of Dubbity's Provost and the senior magistrate
But to have Jock whippèd off to jail full straight.
Guard, do your duty!

GUARD: [*Stepping forward*] Aye, aye, Provost!

JEANNIE: [*Clinging to Jock*] Jock!

MICHAEL: Hold on! Stand still! Or by my wand and
　books

I'll blast the whole black gang of you where you stand!
Put down that pike! [*He makes pass with wand*]

GUARD: Oh! [*He drops his pike as if it burnt him*]

MICHAEL: Now listen to me, my bonnie Provost—
Aye and the good wife too, and you friend Laird.
You made a plot, oh aye, a bonnie plot!
But in your scheming one thing you forgot
This silly warlock! Me!

PROVOST : [*Wildly*] It's all a lie ! Guard !

Take up the warlock too ! As I'm the Provost

I'll have you burnt for this ! In at him, Bellman

Help the Guard grip him. Laird, you watch the door !

Now, in you go !

[*The Bellman, Guard and Provost move to close in on Michael.
Jeannie screams. Michael raises his wand*]

MICHAEL : Stop !

[*The Provost, Lizzie, Guard, and Laird and the Priest
immediately 'stop' in whatever position they were caught by
the wand, then begin to revolve slowly each on his or her own
axis*]

MICHAEL : [*Surprised*] That's queer. [*Shakes wand and puts
it to his ear*].

It seems I've been too free with magic spells

I need recharged !

JEANNIE : What'll we do ?

LAZARUS : Will we run for it, master ?

MICHAEL : No, that'll not help. This clique here'll waken
up

Soon as we leave the room, and then I fear

None of we three will leave the town alive.

We know too much about their villainies !

Let's see now. [*He turns to the magic mirror*] There's still
the glass.

LAZARUS : The magic mirror ? But I thought you said

The devil in it would let no man pass ?

MICHAEL : Aye, so I did, but naught's impossible.

A hero who had no fear might win his way

Even through there and so carve out a road

We all could travel. . . . Who'll be the hero ? . . .

Lazarus ?

[*Lazarus quakes*]

Ah well, it must be Jock.

JOCK : [*Surprised*] Me ?

MICHAEL : Aye, you ! Why not ? I'm sure with your great
    ancestry

Heroism should come entirely natural to you.

JOCK : Have I an ancestry ?

MICHAEL : Going right back to Adam without a break !

Surely you know you're come of the Wallace Wight ?

JOCK : Am I ?

MICHAEL : Indubitably ! and on your mother's side from
    Robert the Bruce.

JOCK : Are you speaking true ?

MICHAEL : As true as heraldry ! Then, going farther back

There's Richard Cœur de Lyon, King Arthur, Lancelot—

JOCK : What ! *Both* of them ?

MICHAEL : Aye, as you'll maybe mind, your most royal
    grand-dam—

Somewhat removed—the fair Queen Guenevere

Wasn't—in some respects—all she might have been.

Then, on your father's side, going farther back

There's Julius Cæsar, Hannibal, Alexander—

JOCK : Alexander the Great ?

MICHAEL : On your father's side. But on your mother's
    side

Away in these distant days—I believe you have

An even more splendid array of hero ancestors—

Hector, Achilles, Joshua—

Aye ! and there was a warrior for you ! Joshua !

David and Jonathan,

Ishmael and oh, but the Lord knows who else more !

JOCK : [*Taking it all in*] Why was I never told about this ?

MICHAEL : Are you certain sure that your mother never mentioned it ?

JOCK : I can't remember. And yet, now that I think of it She often, often called me a bonnie wee prince !

MICHAEL : What did I say ? There, now you've got proof positive !

JOCK : It's true I was never at home with the other lads —As if I was somehow different—kind of superior !

I suppose that would be my noble blood was speaking ?

MICHAEL : That's it. That's it, there isn't a shade of doubt !

JOCK : You know man, when you think of it, it is most damnable

That a man of my descent should be condemned

To herding sheep in old worn clouts like these !

And look at this ! [*Regards his shepherd's crook with disgust*]

Fancy the son of Wallace and the doughty Lancelot—

MICHAEL : [*Interrupting*] On your mother's side.

JOCK : [*Angrily*] What does it matter on whose side it was ?

It's all me isn't it ? Fancy me sporting a thing like this.

It's a sword I should have, a sharp and a shining sword !

[*Shouting*] A sword ! A sword ! Fetch me King Arthur's sword !

JEANNIE : [*Taking sword down from wall and helping him to belt it on*] Here you are, Jock. Take this one.

JOCK : [*Who looks it*] Oh, but I feel so different now !

Do I look different, Jeannie ?

JEANNIE : You look just glorious, Jock !

JOCK : That's how I feel, most glorious, glorious !
  I think my old heart's dead. Here in my breast
  A new heart beats and beats like a drum of war !
  I think it is the heart of the Wallace Wight !
  The heart of Bruce—the heart that the Douglas flung
  Into the bristle of Saracen spears—and died to follow !
  Oh Jeannie ! Jeannie !
  In my blood now yon Cæsar and Alexander
  The noble Lancelot, King Arthur, the brave Achilles,
  Hector and Hannibal and the Hebrew Joshua
  Are all awake. They shout in my inner ear :
  ' Arise, Sir Jock ! Arise take horse and ride !
  Cross thirsty deserts and high mountain ranges,
  Follow long mazy tracks through bogled woodlands,
  Clamber up break-neck cliffs, storm castle walls ;
  Cut off the heads of giants and fiery dragons !
  Break dungeon doors down and set captives free ! '
  [*He draws his sword and flourishes it*]
  A dragon ! Fetch me a dragon !
JEANNIE : [*All in a flutter*] I haven't got one, Jock !
JOCK : Danger ! I must have danger !
  What's the good of being a hero if there's no danger ?
  [*Brandishes sword*]
  Fetch me a dragon ! No ! Bring two—
  One dragon were too simple !
  I'll slay a brace of them for you—
  A dragon for each dimple !
  Bring on your bearded men o' war !
  Your halberts, pikes and bowmen !
  Bring on your highlandmen and all
  I'll lay them all down lowmen !

Now I'm aware of who I am
I'll fight with any de'il, lass !
The Wallace Wight shall nerve the hand,
Achilles keep the heel, lass !
Where is that devil ?

MICHAEL : [*Directing him towards the glass*] This way, Jock !

JOCK : [*Yelling his battle-cry*] Jeannie !

[*Brandishing his sword he charges at the mirror ; the glass
smashes under the sword and he goes battling through*]

MICHAEL : [*Urgently*] After him, Jeannie ! Quick !

JEANNIE : Aye, sir. Wait on me, Jock !

[*She rushes after Jock into mirror*]

MICHAEL : Go on, Lazarus ! They'll waken up soon now.

LAZARUS : What about you, master ?

MICHAEL : I'm coming.

LAZARUS : Don't be long, sir !

MICHAEL : Don't worry about me, lad. Off you go !

[*As Lazarus, reluctantly, goes through mirror, Michael
deliberately begins to remove his shoes. Suddenly the door bursts
open and the dancing bear rushes in. It woofs at the turning
figures then paws at Michael's arm and makes signs towards
the mirror*]

MICHAEL : Ah ! So you want to come too, old hairy-back ?

[*The bear woofs and nods eagerly*]

Well, well, why not ? You too are a friend to wonder.
Away you go through !

[*The bear tries to pull him towards the mirror*]

Aye, aye, I know. I'm coming, coming.

[*The bear shambles out and Michael with his shoes in his hand
walks as far as the frame of the mirror where he turns and
looks back into the room for a moment. Then, raising his*

85

*shoes, he blows a great cloud of dust off them and vanishes.
The turning figures come to life*]

PROVOST: [*Dazedly*] Where are they? Where have they gone?

BELLMAN: They went through there.

[*He rushes at mirror and recoils from glass*] Ow!

PROVOST: They must have got round the back. [*He tears down the velvet hangings and goes round the back of mirror and so out the other side—still in the room*] They're not there either!

PROVOST'S WIFE: [*Suddenly*] Look! [*She points out of window*]

There they are!

PROVOST: Where, Lizzie?

PROVOST'S WIFE: Up there! See! There! Over the old kirk steeple!

BELLMAN: Good God! She's right!

PROVOST: [*Forcibly*] If you ask me there's some damned witchery going on here!

SCENE TWO

The deeps of the sky. Sailing among the stars is an old sailing boat with a patched lugsail. From the top of the mast flies a pennant with the skull and cross-bones. In the bow of the boat lie Jock and Jeannie, in each other's arms ; Lazarus is standing by the mast, holding on to a stay and gazing around him. At the tiller stands Michael Scott.

LAZARUS : Where are we now, sir ?

MICHAEL : Half-way between Fiddler's Green and the Throne of God.

LAZARUS : You mean we're dreaming ?

MICHAEL : Did you just find out ?

LAZARUS : [*Coming astern*] I thought we might be, yet it seems so real.

MICHAEL : Aye, it's a real dream this. We're dreaming true.
There's no need to break your head about it.
Waking or dreaming, it's all one, laddie.
Dubbity's Dubbity whether you take your view of it
From the high church steeple—or the Provost's midden.
Loose the sheet there !
[*Lazarus lets out the sail*]

MICHAEL : That's fine, that's fine. We're soothing along just sweet now.
[*He sings*]
Speed bonnie boat like a bird on the wing
Over the sky to see—
What's the matter with you, Can't you sing ?

87

LAZARUS : [*Seating himself on the gunwale*] I'm not in the
    mood.

    Can I ask you a question ?

MICHAEL : It's your métier as the Frenchies say. Well,
    what is it ?

LAZARUS : This dreaming business. You say we're
    dreaming.

    All right ! Granted we're dreaming, whereabouts in the
    dream are we ?

MICHAEL : I've answered you that. Half-way between
    Fiddler's Green and the Throne of God

    In the point of balance between the opposites,

    Clean clear of necessity.

LAZARUS : Necessesi—what ?

MICHAEL : Material causation or determination, laddie—

    A most damnable heresy that says that B tags A

    C—B, D—C, right down to Z and the end of the alphabet.

    [*A green star passes and he turns to lift his hat to it*]

    Evening, Sirius !

LAZARUS : [*Looking at star*] He looks gye bilious.

MICHAEL : He's green with envy of our foot-free wandering.

    Poor sod ! He's travelled around the same old road

    For a billion years. [*He tries to see round sail*]

    How's the pair in the bow doing ?

LAZARUS : [*Leaning out and seeing Jock and Jeannie kiss*]
    They're doing fine.

MICHAEL : [*Calling*] Hi ! there. Are you all right forrard ?

LAZARUS : They'll not hear you.

MICHAEL : I'll make them hear. [*Loudly*] Jeannie !

    [*Jeannie and Jock look round the sail*]

JEANNIE : Did you say something, Master ?

MICHAEL: I asked were you all well forrard. You're not
    scared are you?

JEANNIE: Why no, since I've Jock beside me, what's to
    fear?

MICHAEL: Naught in the world, lass,—if folk only knew it!
    I just thought maybe you might be wondering
    For what port we're heading.

JEANNIE: I never thought of it. Were you wondering,
    Jock?

JOCK: No me. Does it matter, mister?

MICHAEL: Not a wormed nutshell or a cast clout, laddie!
    Away you go! Hold Jeannie tight. Love on!
    And if I wreck you I'll wreck you upon a star!

JEANNIE: On Venus, Michael.

MICHAEL: Aye, aye, the star of love!
    [*Jock and Jeannie go back to the bow*]
    I like that pair, Lazarus.

LAZARUS: [*Dryly*] Aye, so I've noticed. [*He looks up at the
    sail*] The wind's freshening.

MICHAEL: We'll get there the sooner.

LAZARUS: Where are we going?

MICHAEL: We'll know when we get there.

LAZARUS: Will we ever go back to the earth again?

MICHAEL: We might. The most folk do. But there's
    nothing certain.

LAZARUS: Can I ask you another question?

MICHAEL: Do you ever stop asking questions?

LAZARUS: This one's a wee bit personal!
    Who are you, mister? Oh, I know that you're Michael
    Scott!
    But somehow up here you seem even more than that.

Have you another name, sir ?

[*Michael looks at him for a moment*]

MICHAEL : Take the bar, lad.

[*Lazarus takes the rudder and Michael goes forward and stands with his hand resting on the mast. There is a pause before he speaks.*]

Aye, Lazarus, I've another name,—an immortal name !
And down on the old earth there, a host of names.
Dozens of names ! Dozens and dozens of names !
[*Dreamily*] By Tweeddale side they know me best as
    Merlin.

That was in Arthur's day when folk went out
Cased up like lobsters in bright coats of mail
And worshipped honour. In the German lands
As a lad called Faustus I once raised the de'il—
Aye ! and got hot red hell for it ! I have been
At various times called Nostrodamus,
Zadziel, Albertus Magnus and Paracelsus ;
Among the Greeks, Pythagorous, Orpheus, Hermes ;
Melchior was me—and so was Balthazar !
In Babylon—Now who was I in Babylon ?
Bio—No, that was Thebes. I was Zoroaster !
That was in Bactria. Ha ! I'd forgotten Bactria !
Fancy forgetting Bactria ! The truth is, Lazarus,
I've been so many men I forget the half of them.
Fancy forgetting Bactria ! I've been women too—
But maybe we'd best not speak of that ! I've been a king—
A king ? A whole hand of kings ! I was a pope once.
I've been a Shamen in a Lapland tent,
And friends with cannibals that filed their teeth,
In Russia, Hungary and in old Bohemia

Venetia, Sicily, and in Abyssinia
Been greatly honoured! Aye, and I have been
Burnt in black Spain by the Holy Inquisition
In a yellow robe and a high-peaked dunce's cap
Eight separate times—or was it nine? Oh well
It makes no difference. I aye rose again
Up from the ashes like the Phoenix bird! I have been
Complexioned every colour that skin can turn,
Black, white and saffron, brown and high Indian red,
And all the shades between and the combinations;
Been doctor, barber, alchemist, hermit, friar;
Transmuted metals and brewed true love potions;
Invented a magic wheel, and a brazen head
That answered questions—practised near all professions
Except the law, which I could never abide!
Aye, Lazarus, I've had a host of names.
There's times I wonder who I haven't been
That I can be next!

LAZARUS: Then this isn't the end of you!

MICHAEL: The end of *me*? Of me? I'll never end!
Whenever the world falls back in the weary rut
Worship of dogma or the casual chain
Back to the old brown earth I come again
To break the shackles on imagination!
Confound professors and upset the laws!
Bell out the schools and set young fancies free!
And now do you know me?

LAZARUS: No, master. But I know this
Whoever you are you're the World's Wonder!

MICHAEL: [*Complacently*] That's it, Lazarus. You've got
it now.

LAZARUS : Got what ?

MICHAEL : My——

[*Before Michael can answer a meteor hisses across the sky and through the rigging of the boat. Michael and Lazarus start, Michael grabbing at his hat. The bear which has been asleep, hidden in the bottom of the boat till now, awakes, gets up, and woofs*]

MICHAEL : What the devil was that ?

LAZARUS : It looked like a meteor. [*Pointing down*] Aye. Look ! There she flies !

[*All three, including the bear, hang over the side watching the course of the meteor. Michael straightens himself and sniffs at his beard*]

MICHAEL : Half an inch lower and it would have been no wonder !

[*He scans the boat for damage*]

She didn't damage us, did she ?

LAZARUS : It seems all right back here.

MICHAEL : [*Calling*] Are you all right forrard ?

[*There is no answer and Michael goes forward and looks round sail. Jock and Jeannie have not moved*]

JEANNIE : [*Dreamily*] Aren't the stars lovely, Jock ?

JOCK : [*Fondly*] They're not half so bonnie as you, Jeannie.

JEANNIE : Oh, you're just saying that. You don't really mean it.

JOCK : I do, Jeannie. Honestly I do. Oh, Jeannie, I do love you !

JEANNIE : Oh, Jock !

[*Michael shakes his head over them and returns to the stern where he takes over the rudder again*]

MICHAEL : I don't think they noticed it.

[*He smiles happily*]

Man, Lazarus, when you think of it,

Here in this boat we have the best of life :

Wonder, the love of Wonder, and the Wonder of Love !

[*He looks down over the side and spits*]

To hell with their primar logic ! Lazarus . . .

LAZARUS : Aye, sir ?

MICHAEL : I'm going about now. Watch your head case
    she gibes ! [*Looks down*]

[*He looks overside again*]

MICHAEL : Farewell the world ! Farewell. Mind Michael
    Scott !

Cherish all wonder ; teach the bairns to dream

There's no such riches as imagination.

[*Sharply*] Lazarus !

LAZARUS : Sir !

MICHAEL : Keep watch for comets, meteors, and meteorites.

If we do crack we'll crack on what's material.

LAZARUS : [*Taking look-out position*] Aye, aye, sir !

MICHAEL : I've set a course beyond the last known star.

If we win through we'll burst the bands of space

And beach the morn upon Infinity !

Jet'sun the charts !

[*Lazarus grabs an armful of charts and tosses them overboard*]

LAZARUS : Charts away !

[*The boat, sailing faster and faster passes out of the light
and is lost in the deeps of the sky, while the useless charts
flutter and plunge among the stars*]

THE END

This book is to be returned on or before
the last date stamped below.